NOT A DULL LIFE

RAYMOND D. BRADLEY

VULPINE
P R E S S

Published by Vulpine Press in the United Kingdom in 2018

Cover by Claire Wood

ISBN: 978-1-83919-272-2

www.vulpine-press.com

To those who in the aftermath of my latest life-threatening stroke encouraged me to write this brief autobiography: my sons Gresham and Brett, my brother Murray, and my philosophical colleague, Robert Nola.

FOREWORD

My life has not been a dull one.

Like a multi-hued fabric it has been woven together from threads of different colours and shades:

- My Career in Philosophy;

- My Love of the Great Outdoors;

- My Successes in Ski Racing;

- Women in my Life.

Here I disentangle these four threads in order to tell the stories of each in turn.

THREAD 1: MY CAREER IN PHILOSOPHY

1. INAUSPICIOUS BEGINNINGS

I was a child of the depression: The Great Depression of the 1930s, that is.

Born on 8 December 1930, just over a year after the collapse of Wall Street, the economic reverberations had already begun to take their toll on New Zealand. Unemployment was sweeping across the land. Thousands were on the dole: a paltry benefit available for those who registered. By 1933, when I was just two years old the number of those plunged into poverty was already over 80,000.

My father was one of them. At one time he had been a reasonably successful importer and distributor of Burroughs adding machines, a precursor to today's computers. But demand had collapsed and he found himself without work.

I'm not sure exactly when that was or how long it lasted. I do know that he narrowly escaped the Hawke's Bay earthquake a couple of months after my birth and that he was on a business trip at the time. So, his period on the dole must have been after that. But three years later he was "down and out".

So it was that in 1934, when I was just three years old, we had to move from the comforts of a small bungalow on the outskirts of Epsom in Auckland to a much more modest little house in Jersey

Avenue, Mt Albert. That was just after the death of my maternal grandfather, Guy Thornton, then resident in Fowlds Avenue, Sandringham.

My first clear memories date from about that time.

I remember visiting my maternal grandparents, Guy and his wife Eleanor, on two or three occasions for dinner. I remember going down to feed their "chooks" in the backyard before sitting down to lunch for a midday chicken dinner. It was a special occasion because it was the first time I'd had such a treat. Otherwise the only meat I was familiar with was sheep's heart or tripe (cow's stomach), both served with parsley sauce.

By 5 pm 20 June of 1934 Guy Thornton was dead. Bacillary dysentery was the cause. He had become infected during the First World War when he was New Zealand's first padre with the Anzacs in Egypt. I remember, clearly, visiting on the morning of his death. He was lying in a sunroom with the windows open and white curtains billowing out in a gentle breeze, summoning up strength to pronounce his blessing on his two grandchildren: me and my younger cousin, Sibyl.

I have memories, too, of my paternal grandfather, Ernest Bradley, who died eight months later on 20 February 1935. He and his wife had lived in Birkenhead, accessible by ferry across the Auckland harbour, so our family visits to them were less frequent. Besides, they weren't churchgoers; and my mother had little affection for them.

Both grandfathers had fathers of some note.

Guy Thornton was the son of John Thornton, headmaster of Te Aute Native College for Maori boys from 1878 to 1912. John himself had arrived in New Zealand with his missionary parents three years earlier, in 1875. Many of his graduates, Sir Apirana Ngata, for instance, went on to play an important role in NZ history.

Ernest Bradley was a son of Thomas Bradley who, at the age of twelve, had arrived in New Zealand on the Sir George Seymour late in 1850 (one of the so-called "First Four ships" bringing immigrants to the Canterbury settlement). Thomas went on to become the stationmaster of Lyttleton, reportedly a man much revered by the eight hundred or so railwaymen who attended his funeral.

So much for my recent ancestry. Nothing there to suggest I might lead a relatively eventful and exciting life.

To the extent that anyone gave me and my future a passing thought, they probably would have predicted some sort of career in the church: as a minister, perhaps, or a missionary.

After all, my life was consumed by religious activities: Baptist Harriers (cross-country running) on Saturday afternoons; Young People's Social, on Saturday night; Christian Endeavour, Sunday 10 am; Church Service, Sunday 11 am; Bible Class, Sunday 2 pm; Evening Service, Sunday, 7 pm; plus, annual Bible Class camps; membership of Christian Crusaders at Mt Albert Grammar, etc.

Most of these activities assumed less importance in 1948 when I turned seventeen and began studies at both Auckland Teachers College and Auckland University College (part time). Besides, by this time, my attempts to find a rational justification for my Christian faith had failed and I found myself becoming a covert atheist.

2. EARLY EDUCATION

There was nothing in my early education, primary or secondary, that seemed to offer promise of a successful academic career. I was not an outstanding student in any subject. Except, perhaps, Biology.

Perhaps this was only to be expected. I never understood why my parents moved house so frequently.

- From Epsom, where I was born and lived for couple of years;

- to Jersey Rd., Mt Albert, where I started primary school at Gladstone Road Primary;

- to the beachside suburb of Howick where I attended Howick School for a couple of months;

- to Moana Avenue on the south side of One Tree Hill where I attended Cornwall Park School for two and a half years;

- to Kipling Avenue, Newmarket where I attended the Normal School on Gillies Avenue from halfway through Standard 3 to part way through Standard 6;

- to Fowler Avenue, Mt Albert, from which I cycled daily across Auckland to attend the Normal School again when the army took over our previous location on Gillies Avenue and our class moved to Newmarket.

That was it for the first twelve years of my life: six different residences, five different primary schools.

By the time I started secondary school in 1944 at age thirteen, we had moved again to a house on Alberton Avenue, Mt Albert, right next to Mt Albert Grammar School (MAGS). The constant changes of residences and schools hardly gave me the opportunity to make, and retain, friends or to establish an academic record that was anything out of the ordinary.

Hence it was that upon enrolling in the third form at MAGS, I was relegated to the science stream, widely acknowledged to be inferior to the stream destined for more academically inclined.

3. TERTIARY EDUCATION

I graduated from secondary school in 1947 at age sixteen. No thought was given to the idea of staying on for a second year of the sixth form: after all that was reserved for those who, like my friend Ron Keam, had good reason to envisage a career in a higher profession such as academia. I had no such expectations.

But that was soon to change. In 1948, just after I turned seventeen, I entered the Auckland Teachers Training College in Epsom with the aim of becoming a primary school teacher. And taking the advice of Roy Inglis, himself a noted headmaster and my future father-in-law, I enrolled at Auckland College of the University of New Zealand for part-time studies. He himself had taken part of a BA degree (six units out of nine) in order to give himself an edge when it came to competing with others who were similarly qualified. I should do the same, he argued.

Hence it was that I enrolled as a part-time student at the university, taking courses that were offered after 4:30 pm. After a day's classes at the Teachers Training College.

That was in 1948. I started my university career by taking

5

English stage 1 and first year Biology.

I had a distinguished tutorial teacher in English: the already-famous poet A.R.D. Fairburn. But his tutorials were unproductive in my opinion. I admired his style of delivery: sitting on a desk facing the class and engaging us in animated fashion. But as for intellectual content, I learned almost nothing. I finished the year with a feeling of near contempt for the whole subject. My final grades reflected that. I finished with a percentage mark that nowadays would be classed as a C$^+$ or B$^-$.

Not so with Biology. I had developed a fascination with the subject in the fifth form at MAGS and owed a lot to the advice of my teacher, Peter Ohms, who taught me how to study: not just Biology but other subjects as well.

At the university, there must have been about four hundred students enrolled to listen to the learned lectures of Professor "Barney" (William Roy) McGregor. They were full of substance though somewhat lacking in style. I had no expectations of success. So it was with dismay that I received the news from my good friend and neighbour, lawyer-in-training Barry Holdaway, that he had just seen the ranking of first year students in the final examination and I had come first. (In those days, exam marks were given in percentages and the results were posted on a blackboard in the relevant department.) An A^{++} it would be these days.

In 1949, I started my second year of part-time university studies, still cycling into the university after a full day at the Teachers Training College.

My parents wanted me to take English stage 2. I demurred. That required the study of Old English, a subject in which I had no

6

interest nor, I suspected, any aptitude. I wanted to take Philosophy. But now it was my parent's turn to demur. I might lose my faith, they argued, little knowing that I had no faith left to lose. It took about three weeks before they accepted Barry Holdaway's argument on my behalf that Philosophy stage 1 consisted of Logic and Ethics and that both were religiously neutral. My parents capitulated at the last moment: just in time for me to enrol in the subject that was to become the focus of my whole career.

It was a wise choice, on my part. I finished the year in first place.

I needed to take another subject as well. And Music was my choice. I had already studied piano, then violin, and had developed a passion for classical music that I listened to on the radio, twiddling the knobs with my toes while engaged in other more academic studies.

Music stage 1 required weekly exercises writing harmony for supplied melodies. I worked diligently at ensuring that I was complying with the rules: no consecutive fifths, for example. Some students, more musically gifted than I, took only minutes to complete their tasks; I often took hours.

But my labours paid off. The exam requirements were that one had to pass both of two papers: Harmony, and History and Appreciation of Music. Any mark lower than 50% in Harmony would disqualify one. The Harmony paper came first. I completed less than 50% of the exercises required. Thus, it was an evident truth that I would not, indeed could not, pass Music stage 1 as a whole. So I argued to my mother who, two nights before I was scheduled to sit my first Philosophy paper, persuaded me to spend a little time on preparing for the second music paper. She felt "in her bones," she said, that I should do so.

Her "bones", I was to find out later, were more reliable than my logical reasoning. So it turned out. A couple of weeks after the examinations, I received a call from Professor Horace Hollinrake, head of the music department, inviting me for morning tea. I accepted. He took the occasion to explain that, although I had fallen short of the strict requirements in the examinations, he and fellow Music faculty members had decided to grant me a "pass" on the grounds of the year's exercises well completed. That was a lesson well learned, and much appreciated. I had passed Music as well as Philosophy, albeit having just scraped through the former.

In 1950, having graduated from the Teachers College, I took up an appointment as Probationary Assistant at Edendale School in the Auckland suburb of Sandringham. I was assigned a class of forty-five students. Two of them are memorable: a girl named Patricia who had a remarkable talent for making up and telling Enid Blyton-like stories that held the class spellbound; and a boy named Robert, son of the school caretaker, who couldn't wait until he reached school-leaving age of fifteen and then flaunting his earning power at the meat-works where he found employment: more than double my salary, he boasted, when he rode up alongside me on a powerful new motorbike a few weeks later.

I continued with my night-time university studies, taking Philosophy Stage 2 and Education. Once more my aptitude for Philosophy became evident when I placed first again. I had found my intellectual niche: one that was to become a passion in due course.

Then, in 1951, came a bit of a shock. Having finished my time as a probationary teacher, it was time for me to apply for a permanent post. My hopes of being appointed somewhere in Auckland were dashed: I was given a post at Huntly school, about 60 miles south, thereby rendering continued university studies impossible. I appealed to the Auckland Education Board. They were unswayed. I threatened to resign.

That had the desired effect: they found me a post at New Lynn Primary. By then it was obvious that I had found my intellectual niche. I took Philosophy stage 3 and finished in first place again, and accompanied it with Political Science stage 1. The latter classes were taught by Professor Richard (Dick) Anschutz, head of the Philosophy Department, who infused them with more philosophical content than would be thought normal.

His enthusiasm for the subject led me take Political Science stage 2 extramurally from the University of Victoria in 1952. With that, I had completed the nine "units" that comprised the BA degree.

Hence it was that in 1953 I began taking classes for a master's degree.

Once more I took them as a part-time student while teaching by day, at New Lynn Primary, and attending university at night. Normally, one took them over two years full-time. Especially if one's hopes were for the academic distinction that came with first-class honours.

It was a tough year. But I had the company of another student, Rom Harre, who was teaching by day at a leading secondary school, Kings College. And he, like me, was aspiring to take his master's degree in just one year. We collaborated by passing lecture notes to each other and occasionally discussing them at length. Rom was three years older than me and already held a BSc in mathematics (1948). We both obtained first-class honours. He scored a few marks higher than me, won a scholarship, and went on to Oxford University where he obtained a BPhil and is now widely recognized as a leading contributor to social philosophy.

All this time I was still teaching at New Lynn. My teacher's grading, as assessed by the school inspectors, was the highest for all the male graduates who had graduated from Auckland Teachers College in 1949. Likewise with my teenage sweetheart, Molly, who had graduated from Teachers College at the same time.

But I was becoming disenchanted with school teaching as a career. My disenchantment stemmed largely from disagreements over methodology with the headmaster at New Lynn School: a rednecked intellectual bully of a man, named Evan York, he was more interested in coaching the school rugby team than he was in producing academically successful students.

In January 1954, I married Molly (now known as Adrienne), and continued to consider alternatives to school teaching. One that I took very seriously was a position in New Zealand's Depart of External Affairs. I flew down to Wellington for the interview. Some 212 applicants, I was told.

At the interview, I was given the opportunity to ask some questions. If successful, I wanted to know, what post could I expect? Answer: third secretary. What did that entail? An overseas posting to one of NZ's foreign embassies, was the reply.

Then a hard one addressed to the Head of External Affairs and chairman of the interviewing committee, Alistair Macintosh: What influence, if any, could a senior member of the department such as yourself expect to have over government policy? Alistair referred that one to the most senior member present, Deputy Secretary Foss Shanahan (known as "Foss the Boss" I learned later). Answer: Much depends on the foreign policy of the government in power at the time. In any case the Department of External Affairs could act only in an advisory capacity.

That brought the interview to an end. I was asked to wait outside.

Five or ten minutes later I was invited back in again. And offered the post of third secretary with warm congratulations.

It was not until then that I revealed that my acceptance was conditional on the outcome of another application about which I was expecting to hear in the next few weeks. I had applied for, and was hoping to receive confirmation of, a PhD scholarship in Philosophy at the Australian National University in Canberra, which, if I received it, I would prefer.

I was asked to leave the room again while the committee digested this latest bit of information.

When I returned, Alistair congratulated me on my tentative decision and said that if at any time during the following five years I changed my mind and wanted to accept a post in External Affairs, I should let him know.

In effect, he was offering me a fallback position. Go the academic route if you wish. But if it doesn't work out, the diplomatic route awaits you.

The background to all this requires a little explanation.

4. THE WELLINGTON CONFERENCE

Remember, I had obtained my MA with first-class honours in 1953. But I had nowhere to go other than to stick with my role as primary school teacher at New Lynn. Hence my application to External Affairs. Meantime I kept in touch with the Philosophy Department. And that led to the series of events to which I have just alluded.

I met and became friends with the newly appointed Junior Lecturer, Peter Becroft. Peter had established himself as an outstanding tennis player before accepting a Fulbright Scholarship at the University of California at Los Angeles. There he took his PhD in Philosophy of Science with the prominent German-born philosopher of science, Hans Reichenbach, before returning to Auckland.

It was Peter who was instrumental in having me offered that PhD scholarship at the ANU.

Here is how it happened. Sometime in April 1954, I think it was, Peter told me that he was going to attend and deliver a paper at the forthcoming second Philosophy Conference in Wellington in May. Would I like to join him? After a little thought, and finding that the conference was to be held during the school holidays when I was to be free from my teaching commitments at New Lynn, I said YES.

Later he phoned me to say that Professor Dick Anschutz, head of Auckland's Philosophy Department, had backed out of his prior commitment to contribute a paper, and that the organizer of the conference, Professor George Hughes, was looking for another person from Auckland to replace him.

Why didn't I phone George to offer my services? After a brief discussion with my wife, Molly, I agreed to do so.

I phoned and introduced myself to George as a recent MA graduate from Auckland. Needless to say, he hadn't heard of me. What would the title of my paper be? he asked. Haven't the faintest idea, was my reply. You'd better let me know by Friday, was his. That was the day he'd planned to send out the forthcoming program.

By Thursday, the day before his deadline, I'd made up my mind. The title should be "The Meaning of Freedom", I told him. The notion of free will had captivated me, first, in the theological context of the doctrine of predestination. I now wanted to investigate it in the philosophical context of the doctrine of physical causality.

Then I set to work on writing it. At first, my writing was restricted to nights only as I was still teaching by day. Then the first week of the school holidays, I wrote all day, every day, until the Thursday on which Peter and I took the limited express down to Wellington.

I remember the train trip very well. I was still writing my paper even as the train slowed down for the construction of a new bridge over the Whangaehu River. The previous bridge had been washed away some months before (Christmas Eve, 1953) when a lahar (river of mud) swept down from the crater of the nearby volcano, Mt Ruapehu, with the loss of 151 passengers and crew. The occasion is still referred as "the Tangiwai disaster", Tangiwai being a village nearby.

Peter and I attended the opening session on Friday night and all those on Saturday. I continued writing my paper right up until the Sunday morning when I was scheduled to deliver it. I had so much I wanted to say and so little time to say it.

In attendance was a virtual galaxy of already-established

13

philosophers from Australia as well as New Zealand: John Passmore, Arthur Prior, George Hughes, Jack Smart, Alan Stout, Dan Taylor; and last, but not least, the visiting Oxford philosopher Gilbert Ryle (sometimes described as "The king-maker of philosophy").

I delivered my paper, a version of what is nowadays called compatibilism (that any defensible version of free will is compatible with causal determinism) and received polite applause.

Then I was, so to speak, "thrown to the wolves". For about three quarters of an hour. At the end of which the distinguished logician, Arthur Prior, our chairman, turned to me with the words: "Well, young man, you haven't had much to say for yourself. Is there anything you'd like to say now?" I found his words a little demeaning (though he later said he didn't intend them that way) but struggled to defend myself. At the end, polite applause, again.

It was time for me to make my escape. Or try to. I was nearly out a side door when I was apprehended by someone called Robert Butler who introduced himself as one of Professor John Passmore's doctoral students. He then proceeded to tell me that there were some philosophers who would like him to introduce me in person. They were a group comprising nearly all the aforementioned.

I was introduced to them one by one. Each congratulated me on a great paper, and a great presentation.

In due course, John Passmore explained that he was about to leave the University of Otago to accept a professorship at the Australian National University and offered me a PhD scholarship to study with him. A formal offer of the scholarship, he said, would be forthcoming. (Hence my qualified acceptance of the offer from the

Department of External Affairs.)

Gilbert Ryle capped it all off by saying: "From now on I'd like you to regard me as your philosophical uncle." And philosophical uncle he proved to be, as I shall tell later.

So, it was that a series of serendipitous chances, and a series of equally serendipitous choices launched me on a path to becoming a professional philosopher.

Had it not been for the fact that Dick Anschutz had reneged on his promise to present a paper at the Wellington conference, the opportunity for me to take his place would not have occurred. Had Peter Becroft not told me about the conference and invited me to join him in attending the conference, I certainly would not have attended it. Had Peter not told me of Anschutz's default and suggested that I volunteer to replace him I certainly would not have done so. Had Ron Butler not reached me before I escaped through the side door, I would not have met the supportive group of philosophers or received John Passmore's offer of a PhD scholarship. And so on.

All these chance events and all these contingent choices conspired to get me out of the frustrating career of primary school teaching into the more promising one of an academic career.

But more was to occur before I eventually took up Philosophy as a new profession. I was, after all, a married man with a child on the horizon. The doctoral scholarship from the ANU was generous, but hardly sufficient to support a family of three. This is where serendipity came into play again. A woman named Barbara Fisher who had met me while taking the same MA class, offered me free accommodation in the basement suite of her Remuera residence for the five months before we left for Australia. Her generous offer was thankfully accepted. And so it was that I met her four young daughters one of whom, Juliet (then aged about thirteen), was to play an important role in my later life. As I explain in Part 4, we fell in love in 2001 when I returned from Canada to NZ and lived together happily until she died in August 2015. She had been twice married and twice divorced. And so had I. And we both had two adult children.

5. MY DOCTORAL STUDIES AT THE ANU IN CANBERRA

Molly and I and our young son, Gresham, left for Canberra the following March.

I was not the only PhD student appointed at that time. Eugene Kamenka, son of Russian Jews who had emigrated to Australia from Germany in 1937 when Eugene was only nine, speaking Russian and German but not English, was the other. He was a fast learner, topping English in New South Wales a few years later and then establishing himself as an outstanding journalist, first for the *Jerusalem Post* and then for the *Sydney Morning Herald*. He went on to become a widely respected student of Marx and eventually returned to the ANU to set up a Department of the History of Ideas.

The university supplied all its PhD students with free accommodation in a block of flats. At first Molly and I were in the same block as Eugene before he departed to lecture in Singapore. Then Bob Hawke, destined to be a future Prime Minister of Australia, moved in as a replacement, albeit downstairs.

And I began my studies. In a sense, I had to begin all over

16

again because my studies at Auckland had barely ventured into the twentieth century. G. E. Moore's work in ethics, published in 1908, was as far as we had got. I'd heard nothing of Bertrand Russell or Ludwig Wittgenstein or other major figures of the twentieth century. They weren't even mentioned in passing.

John Passmore was already away in Oxford when we arrived in Canberra, so he could not supervise my studies. He delegated the task of supervising me to Bruce Benjamin, a lecturer at the adjacent Canberra University College. The best Passmore could suggest was that I start by proofreading his new contribution to the history of philosophy: titled *A Hundred Years of Philosophy.* It worked wonders. As I explained before, my philosophical studies at Auckland gave me a thorough understanding of the history of philosophy up to the twentieth century. But not thereafter. Here was the opportunity to bridge the gap to the then-present with the help of one of the greatest historians of the subject. I took up the task with enthusiasm and was rewarded with an acknowledgement of my input in the Preface to his first edition.

By the time Passmore returned to Canberra in 1956, I had already completed my contributions to his forthcoming book and largely made up for the gaps in my knowledge of twentieth century philosophy by reading the works Passmore referred to.

I had also commenced work on my doctoral thesis.

At the direction of Bruce Benjamin, I began by confronting the writings of C. A. Campbell, a Scottish philosopher who was foremost among defenders of the notion of contra-causal free will. The upshot was that I wrote a paper titled "Free Will: Problem or Pseudo-problem" and submitted it to professor Alan (A. K.) Stout, then-editor of the *Australasian Journal of Philosophy*. There was some delay before its publication, as Stout forwarded it to Campbell himself for a reply. Eventually, my paper was published in May 1958 alongside Campbell's "Free Will: A Response to Mr Bradley".

A review of the whole exchange between us became the substance of Chapter 1 of my PhD thesis *Free Will and Logic*.

A second chapter of my thesis focussed on a problem first articulated by Aristotle. Known as the problem of future contingents, it considers a contingent (neither necessarily true nor necessarily false) statement about the future such as "There will be a sea-battle in the Bay of Salamis tomorrow." This was Aristotle's own example.

Prima facie, this statement is either true or false. Consider the possibility that it is true. Then there is no possibility that one could do anything to make it false. Similarly, with the alternative that it is false. Then there is nothing one can do to bring it about that it is true.

By this reasoning the future seems fated: it cannot be other than what it is going to be. I grappled with this in my article "Must the future be what it is going to be?", only with a change of example, and submitted it to the editor of *Mind*, Professor Gilbert Ryle. My example was "Bob Hawke will be Prime Minister of Australia". Ryle published it in *Mind* in 1959.

I had written this in the mid-fifties. Bob did not become prime minister until nearly thirty years later, 1983. Was his becoming PM "fated" ("destined" as I put it before)? Or must we conclude, as Arthur Prior did, that contingent statements about the future are neither true nor false, allowing for the possibility of a so-called "three-valued logic"? (Google tells me that my paper has been cited by thirty-four related articles).

What do you think?

With the publication of these two papers, I had put my foot firmly on the revolving wheel of publication. Hence my paper "Free Will: Problem or Pseudo-problem?" elicited a reply, not only from Professor C. A. Campbell, but also one called "Truth, Futurity, and Contingency" from a philosopher named Peter Wolff. His paper was published in *Mind* 1960.

My paper "Must the Future Be What it is Going to Be?" also elicited a reply from someone named John King-Farlow. It was published in the *Australasian Journal of Philosophy* in 1959. King-Farlow paid a nice tribute to both my original papers when he described them as "two articles of refreshing clarity and vigour".

By the time my scholarship was about to expire towards the end of 1957, I'd almost completed the bulk of my thesis: six chapters pretty much finished; one more to go. I asked for, and was granted, another two years in which to complete.

6. APPOINTMENT TO THE UNIVERSITY OF NEW SOUTH WALES

Completing it would be left until I took up my first appointment at the University of Technology, soon to become the University of New South Wales, in Sydney. Plenty of time, I thought.

Little did I know of the troubles that would befall me.

In the first year, 1958, I had to confront the demands of teaching a huge class, of about 530 students. I stood on a raised platform and delivered my lecture via microphone so as to make

19

myself heard to those at the back of a large lecture hall. Students were required to write three essays. It took me nearly a month to mark each set of them. No time for writing my final chapter.

Worse still was the issue of accommodation. At first, we rented in the suburb of Ashfield. But then we decided to cut expenses by buying a house in Miranda, some miles south of Botany Bay. A cheap house with an outdoor toilet emptied weekly by the "night-cart" man. Making the move took more of my time. Once more, no time for writing the final chapter of my PhD.

Then came my second year at UNSW: 1959. That was to prove even more difficult. Our little house in Miranda was located a few miles west of an oil refinery. The air pollution began to take its toll on Molly's health. Molly had suffered from asthma ever since she was a child. Living in Canberra had afforded some relief. It was located at about 2,000 feet and was relatively free of pollution.

After a few months of living in Miranda Molly's asthma worsened. Her doctor predicted her likely demise within a few months. It was a matter of extreme urgency for us all to move back to Canberra. I say "us all" because by this time we were a family of four, a second boy, Brett, having been born in July 1956. How to make the move?

First, we had to determine whether Molly would indeed get better living back in Canberra. That we put to the test by arranging with some friends, Joy and Frank, to see how Molly took to living with them for a few weeks. After three or four weeks, they reported, she was well enough to help them with the shopping.

Time to sell Miranda and move the family back to Canberra. But where? I persuaded the Registrar at the ANU to let us rent one of the university-owned houses. Then came time to sell the house in Miranda. Meantime, I still had my teaching commitments. My mother came over from New Zealand to look after my boys until the house was sold. I made arrangements with the head of the Philosophy Department to condense my teaching commitments to three days per week. John Thornton, my HOD, was sympathetic: his own wife, Eunice, had died from asthma herself just a few weeks earlier.

The house was sold in a couple of months. Meantime, I had arranged with the University's Bassett College to use one of its bedrooms free for two nights per week in return for giving free tutorials to some of its students.

All that remained was for me make arrangement for transport to and from Canberra each week. During the rest of 1959, I simply drove my VW Kombi van both ways.

But how about that last chapter of my PhD thesis? The whole thesis was due in February 1960. That gave me about two and a half months of vacation in which to complete it.

All was going well: I was hand-writing the final chapter; Molly was taking the manuscript to the typist who returned it to me for proofreading; and the typist would paste the last pages into the back of my already bound theses, three copies of which were required.

Then came near disaster. With about a month to go, I suddenly collapsed with a nasty attack of Meniere's disease: uncontrollable vertigo and ringing of the inner ear. It had hit me without warning. I was sitting at the kitchen table when I suddenly collapsed across the table uncontrollably. Our doctor in Canberra ordered me to bed until I recovered. Complete darkness and quietness, he instructed.

21

Fortunately, I was able to get out of bed in just under two weeks and resume working on my manuscript.

As I remember it, the final deadline for submission of all three copies of my thesis was on Friday 26 February. I drove across Canberra at about 60 miles an hour and got them to the Registrar at the ANU just before 5 pm. He said I needn't have panicked: Monday would have done.

Then back to Sydney to resume my duties. By then I had made new arrangements for my transport between the two cities. I would take the first plane from Canberra to Sydney on Tuesday morning, stay overnight at Basser College on Tuesday and Wednesday nights, then pick up a new Ford on Thursday night and deliver it to the dealership in Canberra later that night. That was how it was supposed to work out.

Occasionally, however, there was no vehicle awaiting me for delivery. And in that case I would have to hitch-hike from Sydney down to Canberra.

One story is worth retelling.

I had hitched my way from Basser College down to the intersection between the Hume Highway (main road to Canberra) and the town of Liverpool. A strong wind was blowing rain horizontally as I stood trying to flag down semis as they sizzled their way past. It was well after 11 pm.

Then to my relief, the headlights of a little VW appeared and slowed down as if destined to pick me up. The passenger door opened up and a voice said, "G'day mate. Where are yuh goin?" I replied, "Trying to get down to Canberra. But if you could get me to Camden I'd be grateful." "Hop in," was the response.

Turned out that the driver was an army mechanic who had already seen me as he was returning to his barracks. "Seen you standing there. Got back to the barracks and thought I'm gonna go for another drive. And there you was, still standing there!"

We were nearing Camden when he said, "Tell you what, mate, I'll take you down to Goulburn." Goulburn is/was about 60 miles from Canberra. We were nearing Goulburn when he said, "Tell you what, mate, I'll take you down to Canberra!"

And so he did. I persuaded him to have some bacon and eggs and coffee, and gave him a few pounds sterling for his petrol before thanking him and sending him on his way back to Sydney.

How's that for going out of one's way for a casual hitch-hiker?

7. MY PHD ORAL EXAMINATION

Sometime later in 1960 I received a phone call from Professor Alan Stout. He was Head of the Moral and Political Philosophy Department at the University of Sydney and was one of my external examiners. The other external examiner, he explained, was Gilbert Ryle, from Oxford. Ryle had delegated to him the task of conducting my oral examination.

Alan said he was flying down from Sydney for the purpose and would be staying at University House on Saturday night.

Did I like whisky, he asked? How about me buying a bottle of Johnnie Walker black label?

Why not, indeed?

The request boded well.

23

Alan was straight to the point. Gilbert and he, he explained, had agreed that I should undoubtedly be awarded my doctorate. Just a few questions that each wanted to ask: Gilbert's about my discussion of quantum physics; Alan's about my treatment of his old friend C.A. Campbell.

Then to the Johnnie Walker. We consumed more than half of the bottle between us. I left the rest with Alan.

My oral examination was over by about 11 pm.

I had my doctorate.

The follow-up came a few weeks later. I heard from the Registrar at the ANU that I had been awarded one of the university's two Post-Doctoral Fellowships. The other had been awarded to a PhD graduate from the Physics Department. I went to Oxford; he went to Cambridge.

8. A POST-DOC PREDICAMENT

There was no question in my mind as to whether or not to accept the Post-Doc offer. But what would happen after that? In the early sixties, academic jobs were few and far between. In a word, they were scarce. John Thornton, head of my department at UNSW, emphasized that. He was making an effort to persuade me to commit myself to returning to the department in 1962 after my spell in Oxford was over.

But that, I pointed out, would still leave me in the predicament of living in Canberra while teaching in Sydney. Better, I argued, to leave the future open rather than commit myself to a continuation of my present problem. True, I might be left without any job at the end of 1961. But I was prepared to take my chances. Accordingly, I resigned from my lectureship at UNSW and made plans to move the whole family to England.

9. MY YEAR IN OXFORD

We made the trip to London in virtual luxury. The ship was Greek, called *Britannia* if I remember correctly. Molly and I had a cabin to ourselves; the boys had a cabin next door and interconnected with ours.

Our ship left from Sydney, travelled via Perth, Singapore, Colombo, and Aden; then via the Suez Canal to Piraeus (outside Athens) and Marseilles, to London.

Perhaps the most memorable events took place during the couple of days while our ship was navigating the Suez Canal from Suez in the south to Port Said in the north. It gave us the opportunity to travel on camels to the Great Pyramid at Giza, then by bus, entertained by belly dancers, to the wonderful Cairo Museum where we saw the mummified remains of various pharaohs, King Tut included, and their glorious golden possessions.

At London docks we were met by my friend Barbara Fisher who took us back to the flat where she was staying with her husband, George, perhaps for the last time, as they were about to separate so that she could pursue her studies at Oxford University while he went back to Auckland. We stayed with them for about three days, then Barbara drove us up to Oxford.

We got to Oxford in time for Hilary term, their second term, which began on Sunday 15 January 1961. Each teaching term was eight weeks in duration followed by liberal periods of vacation. Thus, Hilary term was followed by six weeks of vacation, and the following term, known as Trinity term, was followed by sixteen weeks of vacation before the first term, known as Michaelmas began. Plenty of time for visitors like us to take trips to Europe. More on that in a little while.

Gilbert Ryle had arranged for us to stay with the Macintoshes. Jack was originally from Canada but had done his MA degree in Auckland a few years after me. His wife, Betty, was a New Zealander.

They invited us to share a huge house they had found in the village of Kennington just south of Oxford. We accepted. Unfortunately, the manor-like house, surrounded by over-arching trees, was huge, cold, and very damp. Before long Molly's asthma returned, then turned into pneumonia. It threatened to infect the boys as well. Time to get out.

I found an alternative rental above a bakery on Banbury Road in Summertown just north of Oxford. We moved in and invited Jack and Betty to join us. The house, three stories in all (two above the bakery plus a large cupboard under the stairs) was warm and dry and Molly's health soon recovered.

Jack was doing his BPhil; I was doing my Post-Doc. Both in Philosophy. So, we had plenty to talk about.

And I had lots to do at the university itself. In those days, it was standard practice for leading philosophers to deliver term-long series of lectures on the subjects that they were working on at the time. Thus A. J. (Freddie) Ayer delivered a brilliant series of lectures on probability theory; William Kneale delivered a series on the history of logic; Peter Grice delivered a series on the role of ordinary language; Gilbert Ryle delivered a series on the philosophy of mind; and so on. I attended most of them.

Then there were lectures given by distinguished guests at roughly monthly intervals for the so-called Philosophy Club.

And last but not least, I had to fulfil my commitments as a Philosophy Tutor at Merton College. Once again, Gilbert had arranged that for me. Being a tutor required me to teach five Merton students for an hour each week on a one-by-one basis. I would set a topic drawn from a specified syllabus and get each to write an essay on the assigned topic. Then each would meet with me at an appointed time each week, read his essay and submit to questioning from me. That would normally take an hour or so. Then I'd assign the topic for the following week. And so on it went. Five hours a week for eight weeks.

At the end of two terms I was invited by the Senior Philosophy Tutor for Merton College to meet with him and the Master of Merton prior to dining at high table. The intent was, the Senior Tutor told me, that we would then retire to the Master's quarters where the Master would make me an offer of permanent employment.

Things did not go as planned. Part way through the evening the Master asked me to comment on the performances of each of my five students. Without hesitation, I named X and added that his essays were by far the best: concise, comprehensive, and critical.

The Master sniffed: "But he's so terribly middle class, you know." That provoked me to respond: "Gentlemen, you should know that I come from a working-class background."

That put an end to the evening's conversation. And to my

27

prospect for continued employment. "It's getting so late," the Master said, looking at his Big Ben clock. I never heard a word from either of them again.

It was just as well. I'd talked to Ryle about my fast-fading employment prospects. I'd thought of applying for a job in Singapore. Ryle advised against it. "The heat will kill your philosophical instinct," he said.

Then came news of a Senior Lectureship being available back at the ANU. Above my level, I thought. But then again, why not try?

I did. And I succeeded.

Meantime, again courtesy of good Uncle Gilbert (as I now referred to him), I'd made an appointment to see whether Freddie Ayer would be interested in publishing my thesis *Free Will and Logic*. Freddie liked it and offered to publish it in a Philosophy series he was editing at the time. How long would it take me to polish it up for publication? he asked. I explained that we had plans to take a trip in our Bedford Doormobile van through Spain, France, and Italy for the following six weeks. I'd work on it during that time. Get back to me when you return, was his answer.

But I never did. The trip to Europe got in the way. So did planning to move back to Australia. And so did a recurrence of Molly's asthma. My manuscript was never published. It remains on one of my shelves to this day, barely looked at since 1961. Pity! It really was quite good.

10. BACK TO CANBERRA

I forget the name of the ship we took from London back to Sydney.

Maybe it was *Iberia*, or the *Oriana*.

More significantly, on arrival we took up residence briefly in the home of my future colleague Bruce Benjamin in Canberra. Bruce and family had commissioned a magnificent house from the highly regarded Czechoslovakian architect Alex Jelinek who practised from Melbourne. Popularly referred to as "The Round House", it won "The House of the Year for 1957". We had the honour of living in it, free of charge, for six weeks until Bruce returned from a six-week trip to Oxford where he had taken over my Bedford Doormobile before we departed.

Bruce, you may remember, had been my supervisor in Passmore's absence. By the time he returned from Oxford I had been able to rent a house from the ANU on Cobby St. just above the National Museum of Australia. He was already Senior Lecturer of Philosophy in the School of General Studies of the ANU. I joined him there in the same capacity.

The Head of our department at that time was the distinguished moral philosopher, Professor Kurt Baier. Kurt wanted me to teach first year logic and recommended Peter Strawson's text *Introduction to Logical Theory*. I demurred and argued instead for an approach that I had learned from my ex-colleague, Charles Hamblin, at the UNSW, one that put the emphasis on modal logic: logic featuring the notions of necessity, possibility, impossibility, and contingency. Kurt eventually agreed, especially when I told him that Arthur Prior, perhaps the world's greatest logician of the time, held Charles in high regard for his work on modal logic.

I went on, years later, to develop that approach in *Possible Worlds: An Introduction to Logic and its Philosophy*, co-authored

29

with my colleague Norman Swartz.

During my first year I was challenged to my first formal debate ever: by a Dominican priest who was taking one of my courses in Philosophy. My main thesis was that many of the principal beliefs of Christianity, beliefs regarded as central to its status, were both "morally obnoxious" and "intellectually pernicious". My opponent, of course, argued for the contrary. I was voted the clear winner.

Meantime, two events occurred that changed the complex of the School of General Studies. First, Kurt Baier went off to the University of Pittsburgh and was replaced by another ex-Austrian, Peter Herbst. Second, my close friend, Bruce Benjamin, died of prostate cancer in March 1963.

11. ANOTHER WELLINGTON CONFERENCE

Later that year, Peter Herbst suggested that he and I offered to read papers at the forthcoming Philosophy Conference in Wellington. I leapt at the chance. It would give me an opportunity to see my parents, brothers, and friends again. Besides, attending a Wellington conference had been good for my career back in 1954. Who knew how good it might prove to be nine years later? I certainly had no idea.

I chose to deliver a paper titled "Geometry and Necessary Truth" scheduled to be published in *The Philosophical Review* in January 1964. My paper was very well received, and I was urged to apply for the chair of Philosophy at Auckland. I was surprised to hear that it was vacant: that Anschutz had retired at the end of 1961 and that his position had been filled since then, first by Pflaum on a

30

temporary basis, and then by the retired Scottish Professor Alexander MacBeath who was one of the authors of the text *The Elements of Logic* I had studied in first year. MacBeath himself was one of the keenest of my supporters. So was George Hughes, as he had been once before in 1954.

A week or two later I submitted my application. I had several competitors, mainly from Australia and one at least from Canada. The interview by the University Appointments Committee was gruelling. But eventually I heard that I had succeeded: I had been appointed to the Chair of Philosophy at the University of Auckland.

It was time to pack up once again.

12. THE PHILOSOPHY DEPARTMENT AT AUCKLAND

I'll let Gavin Ardley (Senior Lecturer during my time) put my time at Auckland in perspective. In his monograph *Sixty Years of Philosophy: A Short History of the Auckland University Philosophy Department 1921-1983*, he wrote:

Chapter 7
Professor R.D. Bradley

In the six years of the Bradley regimen the department went through a revolutionary transformation. A number of elements combined to accelerate the process…

To be productive of revolution they needed an *animateur*, as the French say. This was provided by the dynamic character of the young professor – he was 33 years of age when appointed to office.

It was an exciting time. Reforms previously unthinkable were carried out with such *elan* that they secured ready co-operation. If some of the experiments proved to be over-ambitious, much of what was done was sound and enduring. The Department physically was moved out of the Old Arts building to a house of its own at the corner of Wynyard and Havelock Streets (where Human Sciences now stands). A spirit of enthusiasm captured the students. A corporate atmosphere was created; a common tea-room helped to bridge the gulf between staff and students; the tutorial system prospered; the student philosophical society and refreshment of visitors kept everyone alert. Activating all, seen by all, here there and everywhere, was the athletic figure of the professor...

As well as his academic attainments, Ray Bradley's energies overflowed into the sporting field: an intrepid captain of skiing, a penchant for fast cars, feats of bicycling. He could not but be the cynosure of students. If anyone could reform a sedate department it was Bradley.

I'll take up the story again at this point.

The department I inherited was almost totally different from the one I'd left in 1954. Just one faculty member remained: Bernard Pflaum. Bernard was still the Senior Lecturer he'd been when he taught me in Stage 1 Philosophy. He was a good man who taught well and had a lot of sympathy for his students.

My first task was to change the curriculum from one pre-occupied with Philosophy prior to the twentieth century to one that included such twentieth century figures as Bertrand Russell and Ludwig Wittgenstein. I managed to engender enthusiasm for these revolutionary ideas.

That was just one of the new ideas I introduced. I introduced the hitherto *verboten* subject of Philosophy of Religion, a course in Political Philosophy, two courses in Contemporary Philosophy, a highly organized student seminar (modelled on the Oxford system), etc.

In my first year, 1964, I was approached by the Anglican chaplain to see whether I would be interested in holding a series of debates (ten in all) over the Winter term with the distinguished Christian, Botany Professor Val Chapman, on topics in the Christian Religion. Seems that the chaplain had heard about my debate with the Dominican priest in Canberra in 1963. Such discussions of religion had long been taboo in NZ academia. I accepted the challenge, and by popular vote seemingly won.

The following year, 1965, I was pitted against a much more formidable opponent, the University Orator and Professor of Classics, Professor E.M. Blaiklock. (I had held private discussions on religion with Blaiklock when I was about fifteen and he was a member and occasional lay-preacher at the Baptist Church I was attending at that time.) In the final session, out of ten in the series, up to 900 students and staff were in attendance. It was probably a draw, though my own students thought I had won overall.

That was enough on public debates on religion.

Though not on politics. In May 1965, I learned that the Holyoake cabinet was about to yield to US pressure by sending a battery of New Zealand artillery to Vietnam. I was strongly opposed to the move and sent a telegram to the prime minister to that effect. I had sought the support of Bob Chapman (Politics) and Keith Sinclair (History), but both desisted, preferring instead to make the case against NZ involvement in the *Herald* newspaper. Keith did so some months later, when it was too late. But Bob did never did.

Two years later, I took a sabbatical, starting in August 1967. Molly and I spent about three months in the USA, two in Canada, and one in the UK before returning to NZ via Scandinavia, Finland, the Soviet Union, Afghanistan, India, Thailand, Cambodia, Hong Kong, and Australia. I presented about twenty papers in North America and was offered about eight professorial posts, the most prestigious being as a replacement for Professor Maurice Mandelbaum at Johns Hopkins University.

I hadn't invited any of these invitations, so declined all of them and returned to New Zealand in May 1968.

But the new horizons these invitations opened up set Molly and me thinking about the future. Should we stay in Auckland until retirement: another thirty or so years? Or should we yield to one of the prospects that had been offered to me? One thing was clear. The USA, though attractive in many ways, was not an option: not just because of my own opposition to its foreign policy, but because of the likelihood of at least one of my boys being recruited into the military.

That left Canada alone as a plausible candidate.

The next Christmas, 1969, I took a month-long holiday in Canada, retracing my steps and reassessing my options. I delivered a paper on the philosophy of arithmetic (subsequently published as "Must the propositions of Arithmetic be Empirical?" in *Nous*) that I had written jointly with Malcolm Rennie, a brilliant young logician whom I had recruited from Australia.

I had several professorial appointments dangled before me

34

again: at the University of Calgary, the University of Manitoba, the University of Victoria (on Vancouver Island), and Simon Fraser.

The offer that attracted me most was at Simon Fraser University. But there I found myself up against Jonathan Bennett, another New Zealander who had taught me a course on Spinoza in Auckland and then had gone on to a distinguished career at Cambridge.

The SFU Appointments Committee asked my opinion as to whom they should appoint. I said they should appoint Jonathan if they wanted the best philosopher, me if they wanted someone with more experience as a Head of Department who could be trusted to hold the department together.

They appointed Jonathan. And I returned to Auckland.

Then, about half way through 1969, I heard from Jonathan. He was having problems with the faculty. As I'd guessed he would. Would I like to accept a post as fellow-Professor so that he could leave at the end of the year (1970) for a post across Vancouver at the University of British Columbia?

Once again, Molly and I deliberated about the offer at length. Then we decided. We'd go to Vancouver. Not only would that give me an opportunity to put into practice some of the ideas I had for operating a Philosophy Department, it would also give us the opportunity to indulge our other two passions: one for living in the wilderness; the other for skiing.

Off we went again. On an ocean liner, the *Canberra*, via Honolulu to Vancouver.

13. SIMON FRASER UNIVERSITY

On arrival in January 1970, we accepted the offer of a future colleague and friend, John Tietz and his wife Grace, to move into their house in Burnaby for three weeks or so while we searched for our own accommodation.

It proved disastrous. Little did I know, at the time of accepting John's generous offer, that their house was located only a few miles from the oil refineries in Port Moody.

The proximity took its toll on Molly's health almost immediately. (Shades of our time at Miranda close to the oil refineries on Botany Bay!)

By the time I'd located a suitable house in West Vancouver, I had to carry her from the agent's car in my arms to see it. Fortunately, the house was already empty having been vacated by its owners who had left to live in Florida some weeks previously. They were eager to sell and accepted my low-ball offer. The house, on Roseberry Avenue, was just below the motorway leading to the ferry terminal on Howe Sound. It was also located just above the pollution level that rose and fell in surges above Burrard Inlet about six hundred feet below.

Molly's asthma disappeared within weeks of our taking up residence. (As it had previously when she moved back to the clear air of Canberra from smoke-laden Miranda back in 1961.)

The house was magnificently located on the lower slopes of one of the south-facing North Shore Mountains, Mt. Hollyburn. We looked down across Burrard Inlet to Vancouver with the Olympic Mountains of Washington State on the horizon. To the west lay the mountains of Vancouver Island and to the east was 1200 feet high Burnaby Mountain with Simon Fraser University straddling its peak.

The fact that it was located about twenty-three miles west of Simon University Fraser was neither here nor there. I could make the trip from home to the university in about half an hour.

The university had been designed by esteemed architects Arthur Ericson and Geoffrey Massey and was ready for occupation in September 1965, just over four years before I arrived. It was still going through growing pains: student unrest culminating in student occupation of the President's office, and RCMP arrest of many of the protesters.

Because I'd been on the Senate of Auckland University at a time when we had narrowly averted similar problems, I was invited to advise the newly appointed President, Kenneth Strand, as to how to handle student protest and the supporters they'd garnered from young staff members, principally from the Department of Politics.

I spent many evenings in discussion with Ken in the President's office. How should we handle the protesters, especially those from the Department of Politics, Sociology, and Anthropology whose cases for tenure were about to be heard by the University Tenure Committee of which I was a leading member? How should we handle members of the press who were only too eager to make the case for dissident staff and students?

I remember the case I made when I and the Dean of Arts were questioned on the radio by an aggressive journalist. He caught me out at one point when I dismissed one of his questions, by starting with, "No problem." That wasn't an appropriate thing to say when we'd been invited to talk about the *problem* the university was

37

having at the very time when we were talking.

This was a hard beginning. And it went on for a couple of years. It wasn't surprising given my background and experience when compared with that of other senior members of the University Senate. There were others, older than me, but none of them had experience that equalled mine.

I could go on telling in detail the story of my academic career at Simon Fraser between January 1970 when it started to the date when it ended in May 1996. At that time, retirement at age 65 was mandatory. I had made that age after twenty-seven years of working in SFU. A lot can occur in that time. So, I'll content myself with emphasising some of the most significant.

Some of my administrative appointments were at the Faculty level. For example, I was appointed to the Faculty of Arts Committee in an advisory capacity to the Dean of Arts. Others were at the Senate level. For example, I was appointed to the Senate Academic Committee, responsible for sanctioning all new appointments. I started as a member of this committee; then was appointed to the position of Chairman.

I was appointed as the university's member of the nation-wide committee for making grants to members of the Arts faculty, Social Sciences and Humanities council of Canada (SSHRC). Later, I took the role of Chairman.

And last but not least, I joined Brian Wilson, Academic Vice-President and a close friend of mine as one of the two representatives of Simon Fraser on the Academic Board of Higher Education. This was a committee comprising a Chairman from the Provincial Department of Education plus two members each from the province's three universities. Our role was to advise the Minister of Education on the development of tertiary education facilities in the province. In that capacity Brian and I took several flights around the province to help steer various colleges that were aspiring to have their courses accepted by the universities in the right direction. I think it fair to say that Brian and I were the most prominent and influential of the Committee's members: we certainly were so regarded by the Chairman.

All this took an inordinate amount of my time over a period of about ten years. So, when I was asked by the university Registrar, to consider accepting some other administrative role, I declined.

Not only that: I also handed in my resignation from the whole damned lot. The Registrar had explained that many senior faculty members had viewed me as a future candidate for the role of University President. I thought about that for a couple of weeks, then decided that I had no such ambitions. I wanted, I explained, to get back into publishing Philosophy as was my intent when I accepted the role of Professor in the first place.

Meantime, I had not been entirely unproductive. When I took up the job at SFU, I undertook to teach first year Logic and wrote some notes for my students. They were akin to those I'd distributed to first year Logic students at Auckland. One of my colleagues, Norman Swartz, liked them and suggested we write a book together incorporating my notes together with stuff on modal logic at the end.

After a year or so, we decided on an entirely new approach, making the stuff on modal logic foundational at the beginning. We worked on it together for several years and came up with a fresh approach to the whole subject. We titled it *Possible Worlds: An*

Introduction to Logic and its Philosophy, then submitted it for publication. Our chosen publishers were Basil Blackwell publisher (in Great Britain) and Hackett Publishing Company, Inc. (in the United States of America). The book (published in 1979) was the forerunner of many other texts the authors of which paid tribute to our innovation. Thus, Paul Herrick, the author of *The Many Worlds of Logic: A Philosophical Introduction* published by Harcourt Brace five years later (1994) wrote:

> My greatest debt is to the text *Possible Worlds* by Raymond Bradley and Norman Swartz. Many of my pedagogical ideas developed as I taught with that excellent book.

Our book, according to reports, was still in use around the world over fifteen years later. To this day, it is still available free of charge at *Amazon.com.*

For a few years I limited my publications to learned journals. Then I resumed book publications with an edited volume of conference papers: *Environmental Ethics, Volume II*, co-edited with Stephen Duguid, published by Simon Fraser University, Institute for the Humanities, 1989.

Volume I, edited by my colleague Philip Hanson, had been published three years earlier. Both volumes were members of a series focussing on matters of public interest and concern.

Another instance was the volume *Pornography and Censorship: New Concepts in Human Sexuality*, co-edited by my then-colleagues Susan Wendell and David Copp, and published by Prometheus Books 1983.

All three, plus others whose titles I now forget, were responses

40

to my urging the department to expand its scope to issues of social policy. Conferences were held annually, papers were contributed by prominent authors, and printed by established publishers. Their success can be gauged by the reception they received from the public at large and from the fact that student enrolments in Philosophy at SFU rose markedly at a time when those of other Philosophy Departments were reportedly dropping around North America.

It is one of those things the likes of which I had envisioned while still at Auckland but had not had time to enact before departing for SFU.

A few years later, I published a book on the early thinking of Ludwig Wittgenstein, *The Nature of All Being: A Study of Wittgenstein's Modal Atomism,* (Oxford University Press, 1992).

I'd begun thinking carefully about Wittgenstein's work *Tractatus Logico-Philosophicus* back in my days at Auckland. I thought then that a good case could be made for identifying his views with those of Bertrand Russell whose lectures on *The Philosophy of Logical Atomism* he credited to his pupil, the young Wittgenstein. Having come to that conclusion, I had ignored most of Wittgenstein's *Tractatus* in classes and substituted the much more readable lectures of Russell.

Yet over the years I came to the conclusion that a more careful reading of Wittgenstein's early work, in particular his *Notebooks 1914-1916,* led to a very different interpretation. The title of my book derives from an epigraph from the *Notebooks,* written 22 January 1915:

My whole task consists in giving the nature of the

41

proposition. In giving the nature of all being. (And here being does not stand for existence.)

But what does this mean? I argued that an account of modality lies at the very centre of the Tractarian metaphysics. And that his account is superior in many ways to those of contemporaries such as Adams, Carnap, David Lewis, Rescher, Stalnaker, and above all David Armstrong. I was particularly happy, therefore, when Armstrong began his review (in *Notre Dame Journal of Formal Logic*, Winter 1993) with the words:

> This is an excellent book. It will interest both students of the *Tractatus* and philosophers who consider the metaphysics of modality.

Armstrong ended his review by saying:

> Bradley gives us a bold and novel reading of the modal views espoused in the *Tractatus*. He also does a very useful job in comparing and contrasting this position with later accounts of the metaphysics of modality. His arguments are not, in my opinion, always convincing. But that's philosophy.

I agree with his ending words. Disagreement is, indeed, the very essence of Philosophy.

My book, *The Nature of All Being*, was published just four years before I retired in 1996.

By then I'd also published about forty-five philosophical articles in reference journals such as *Mind*, *The Australasian Journal of Philosophy*, *Sophia*, *The British Journal for Philosophy of Science*, *Nous*, *Dialogue*, *The Canadian Journal of Philosophy*. My subjects

42

ranged over Metaphysics, Determinism, Fatalism, Free Will, Ethics, Philosophy of Religion, Philosophy of Science, Philosophy of Quantum Mechanics, Epistemology, and Philosophy of Logic.

My post-retirement articles included nine in *The Secular Web* (several of which were subsequently anthologized), four articles on the Philosophy of Einstein, and five articles on issues associated with time for *The Encyclopedia of Time: Science, Philosophy, Theology and Culture* (2009). For access to these, many in pdf format, use your search engine to find "Ray Bradley, Philosopher".

My last book was titled *God's Gravediggers: Why No Deity Exists* (Ockham Publishing, UK, 2015). It has been described as a *coup de grace to religion* making use of logical, scientific and moral arguments; "a timely book in an age of religious fundamentalism, hatred, and conflict." Reviewers include:

Professor Robert Nola (University of Auckland):

> From a young person's rejection of Christianity, to a mature philosopher's critique of all religion. This compelling defense of atheism is a brilliant read.

Theodore Drange (West Virginia University):

> Bradley's forte is logic and he brings that to bear throughout the work. It is well-written and thoroughly absorbing. I have nothing but praise for his project.

Ex-Christian turned Atheist, John Loftus:

> This book of Bradley's in one I compare to the late Michael Martin's book, "The Case Against Christianity" (1995). I highly recommend them both, although I prefer "God's Gravediggers".

43

Someone identifying himself as "Still Christian":

> I would count this book as up there with some of Mackie's work as far as academic rigor is concerned, and with Ingersoll and Hitchens as far as eloquence and sheer argumentative skill is concerned.

I submit that that's not a bad note on which to near the end of one's post-academic career.

14. CONFRONTING EVANGELICAL CHRISTIANS IN ORAL DEBATE

Two chapters from *God's Gravediggers* are elaborations of arguments I first presented in oral debate some twenty or more years before. Chapter 5 "The Moral Argument for Atheism" enlarges on a debate I had with Dr. Paul Chamberlain from an evangelical Vancouver Bible College in 1994. Chapter 6 "The Logic of Hell and Damnation" enlarges on a debate I had with highly esteemed Dr. William Lane Craig in 1995.

Here I sketch the content of each debate and the outcome of each.

A. The debate with Chamberlain was over the question: "Can there be an objective morality without God?"

Clearly, for our debate to be a genuine one not a merely verbal one, it was important for us to agree on the meaning of the central terms involved. We agreed, therefore that by "objective moral truths" we would mean - as *The Dictionary of Philosophy* defines it - "moral

44

truths which would remain true whatever anyone or everyone thought or desired." Examples I submitted included:

P1. It is morally wrong to murder (wantonly slaughter) innocent men, women, and children.

P2. It is morally wrong to provide one's troops with young women captives so that they can be used as sex-slaves.

P3. It is morally wrong to take revenge on your enemies by having their wives raped and their children dashed to pieces before their parents' eyes.

P4. It is morally wrong to demoralize people by making them cannibalise their own children.

P5. It is morally wrong to offer people as sacrifices, by burning or otherwise.

P6. It is morally wrong to torture people for holding beliefs different from your own.

Chamberlain argued for a negative answer to our main question: "Can there be an objective morality without God?" He claimed that that the biblical god exists and that if he doesn't there could be no objective moral truths.

I argued to the contrary (a) that there can be objective moral ethics in the absence of any God whatever, and further (b) that the existence of objective moral truths requires the non-existence of the biblical God.

Re (a), I pointed out that there are many ethical theories that would provide the ground for upholding these principles as objective moral truths: Kantian ethics, and Utilitarianism are just two examples.

Re (b), I cited biblical texts in which God is depicted as violating each of our examples.

In our subsequent discussion, Chamberlain seemed taken aback by coming up against an opponent who was able to cite chapter and verse of the Bible.

So were many of his would-be supporters in the audience. One of them, a certain Professor Hector Hammerley from the Department of Linguistics at Simon Fraser University, was so incensed that he tried to get back at me on God's behalf by crossing over the border into that gun-ridden country, the USA, and purchasing a hand gun with which to shoot me. Fortunately, for him as well as me, he was arrested by the RCMP when he attempted to return to Canada with his newly purchased weapon.

So the Dean of Arts at SFU told me some time later.

Hammerley's planned action befitted that of the biblical God he was trying to defend.

B. My debate with William Lane Craig, representing *The Campus Crusade for Christ*, was of a very different character. It was eminently rational.

It was reviewed by Luke Muehlhauser in the now-defunct website for Common Sense Atheism under the title "William Lane Craig vs. Ray Bradley". Luke himself was an evangelical Christian until, at the age of twenty-one he began to study the Historical Jesus and, in January 2008, lost his faith.

Under the heading "William Lane Craig's Debates" he reviews nearly fifty of Craig's pre-2009 debates, including mine. He begins by paying a tribute to Craig who he describes thus:

> William Lane Craig is a prolific Christian philosopher, apologist, author, and public debater. He is the best debater – on *any* topic - that I've ever heard. As far as I can tell, **he has won nearly all his debates with atheists**.

It would seem that, in his view, I and another philosopher, Keith Parsons, are exceptions.

Of my 1964 debate he writes: "One of my favourite atheism vs theism debates is the one between Ray Bradley and William Lane Craig on the doctrine of hell".

He summarises the review by writing:

> How can a good God torture forever those who've never heard of him? This is a hard question for Craig to answer, and Bradley is a good debater – on both the emotional and intellectual levels. This might be a debate that Craig lost.

He concludes his review with:

> Bradley was, unlike nearly all of Craig's opponents, *prepared*. He had read Craig's work on the topic. He responded *directly* to Craig's points and offered *specific rebuttals* and *counterarguments*. All this is nearly *unheard of* among atheist debaters of Craig. Moreover, Bradley was rhetorically effective and nearly as concise as Craig. **Ray Bradley is perhaps the best atheist debater I've seen, and it's a shame he hasn't done more debates!**

Clearly, Muehlhauser knew nothing of the debates I'd held with evangelical Christians some thirty plus years before: in Australia in

1962 and New Zealand in 1964 and 1965, totalling thirty-one in all. Not surprising: he wasn't born until sometime in 1963. And I could hardly expect my earlier reputation as an atheist debater to last until 2008 when he wrote his assessment of my debate with Craig. After all, even the countries were different.

Muehlhauser pays a similar tribute to Keith Parsons of whose 1998 debate with Craig "Why I am or am not a Christian" he writes:

> This is the other debate Craig may have lost. He certainly lost it on logic, though he probably won on rhetoric and organization (as he always does). Parsons is full of logic, common sense, and passion.

I'm happy to be ranked more or less alongside Keith Parsons whose argumentative skill I much admire.

Raymond
Bradley,
circa 1980

Raymond Bradley,
circa 2010

Raymond Bradley, circa 1980

THREAD 2: MY LOVE OF THE GREAT OUTDOORS

1. VISITS TO WAIMANGU VALLEY, NZ

In some ways my love of the great outdoors began with events stemming from a precise place and date: a visit to Waimangu (near the centre of the North Island of New Zealand) on 18 January 1951. It was then that my friend, Ron Keam, and I cycled about 25 km from Rotorua to the tourist resort of the world's youngest geothermal system in Waimangu Valley. And back again. We did that two days in a row.

Waimangu Valley itself was created during the volcanic eruption of Mt Tarawera on 10 June 1886.

Our visit came about this way. My parents had decided to take the family – myself, Neville and Murray – down to Rotorua for holiday and asked me if I'd like to bring a friend. I chose Ron Keam who had already accompanied me on several rambles through the Waitakere Ranges, just west of Auckland. I had learned of Ron's fascination with NZ's principal thermal area, so it was natural for me to bring him along.

We were to make the visit to Waimangu repeatedly, helping to establish some of the valley's acclaimed walking trails. Our first visit was celebrated by the then-current owners some sixty years later, in our presence. We had followed up the visit of 18 January 1951 with many similar visits, going down the valley filled with near-boiling water (Frying Pan Flat, the largest hot spring in the world), jumping over the hot stream that drained it, climbing up what was popularly called "Gibraltar Rock" on the far side, jostling my way across the narrow neck of steaming cliffs that led to the main structure, (reputedly the first person to have done so up to that time, though a park employee – I have been told - duplicated my feat some twenty odd years later). We climbed up into Inferno Crater Lake (the largest geyser-like feature in the world), up to and down into Fairy Crater and Black Crater, and so on, usually finishing up on the shores of Lake Rotomahana (under which are buried the remnants of the famous Blue and White Terraces), before returning up the valley to our starting point.

That was the beginning of a life-long love of the great outdoors, not only for me but for Ron especially. In his case it issued in the publication of his wonderful volume *Tarawera: The Volcanic Eruption of 10 June 1886* (published in 1988 while he was still a Professor of Physics at Auckland University).

In my case, it issued in an enduring love of outdoor life that lasted with me during my time in Australia and Canada; and back to New Zealand again.

2. Joining Canberra Alpine Club

When Molly and I arrived in Canberra in March 1955, it was natural for us to seek an outlet for our outdoors passion. To the west lay the Brindabella Ranges, with peaks such as Mt Franklin, Mt Ginini, and Mt Gingera, etched on the skyline up to 6,000 feet or so. We sought, and found, friends in the Canberra Alpine Club (CAC).

It appealed to us to learn that the Club had a ski club that had been established back in 1934. We joined.

Membership of the CAC widened our circle of friends beyond those of the ANU to people in the wider community. The population of Canberra at the time was just over 29,000. We got to know and spend time with people in all walks of life. Among the most memorable are the manager of the Commonwealth Savings Bank and his wife, the Manager of Port Kembla Steel Works and his wife, a prominent journalist, a French polisher and his wife, an economist working for the Federal Government, a car mechanic, a ski salesman and his wife, several immigrants from Eastern Europe, and so on. We socialized with them at people's homes, at yearly banquets, and most importantly at the ski chalet on Mt Franklin. That's where we learned to ski. Sort of.

Our equipment at that time was extremely primitive. Molly was pregnant with our second child, Brett. Somehow, I came to have a pair of 215 cm solid hickory Marius Eriksen manufactured in 1938. They lacked edges until I chiselled out channels and screwed in some interlocking steel edges. They also lacked modern safety bindings, being equipped with so-called bear-trap bindings, with spring-loaded heel clips, and long-thong leather straps to tie one's boots in.

My boots were worse. Pre-war, too. Ill fitting, leather made, and stiff. Hardly a weekend went by without me coming home with my socks soaked in blood.

But we loved our weekends up at the chalet. Driving up there took about one and a half hours in our little Fiat 500 station wagon. Much depended on the snow conditions. We tried to be first in the queue, relying on other club members to lift us out of the way if we got stuck. Our car was light. No problem for a few robust skiers. Especially if they were soldiers from the Royal Military College (RMC) in Duntroon grinding their way in a huge 4-wheel drive truck wanting to make their way further along the Brindabella range to their own ski hut, past Mt Ginini, and to the still more distant Mt Gingera.

Driving up to the Mt Franklin road, we often came across herds of kangaroos and the occasional wombat. Then to the Canberra Alpine Club chalet itself. The chalet had been built in 1938 with an asbestos cement roof to protect it from forest fires, but not from snow flurries that were apt to blow in under the eaves. It had rooms for over thirty people located upstairs, with a large cast iron wood stove and an open fireplace downstairs. Frequently we woke to find our sleeping bags covered with a fine powdering of snow.

The chalet was located at the bottom of a firebreak providing access to the summit of Mt Franklin a few hundred feet higher. Molly and I carried our sons up the track along with packs, ski, poles, and a groundsheet to the peak where we would install the boys in the shade of a large gum tree. One of us would look after the boys while the other would make attempts to ski down the hand-hewn ski runs below.

Ski technique at that time was an issue of hot debate. The Arlberg method, which emphasized a gradual progression from snow ploughs, through stem christies, and eventually to parallels? Or the new French method, as espoused by the great French racer

Emile Allais, which made the move to parallels directly by emphasizing a hop-like movement which the French called the "ruades"? I tried both. Most of my European friends, like the Hungarian skier George Haynod and the Pole Jan Gdowski, encouraged me to ski the Arlberg way; a beautifully illustrated book by Allais encouraged me to progress straight to parallel skiing. Result? It took me a full year to learn to turn to the left; another year to turn to the right. Only in my third year did I put the two together so as to ski through bamboo poles in a ski race.

July 1956 was a memorable year for snow. The winding road from Piccadilly Circus (at the top of the Brindabella range) to Mt Franklin was buried in deep snow preventing even the RMC trucks from making headway. A group of club members congregated at Piccadilly Circus debating what to do. Did anyone want to walk the 20-odd km to the chalet or would we all go home? A fellow member, named Bruce Bray, volunteered to join me in making the journey. Perhaps the fact that we were able to take short cuts up firebreaks made the trip a little shorter. But we were slowed down by the fact that we were wearing skis and carrying packs loaded with food, sleeping bags, etc. At all events, it was well after dark by the time we reached our objective, unlocked the hut, and started the fire. Next day, of course, we had to repeat the trip in reverse.

But it was well worth it. We were climbing silently up a mountain close by Mt Franklin when we came upon a huge red kangaroo (about 6 foot tall we estimated) feeding silently on the mosses and grasses that the recent wind storm had exposed under the roots of a huge fallen gum. We were just feet away before it sensed our presence. With huge silent jumps it bounded away through the deep snow into the darkening bushes. A memorable experience for us

55

both. And, possibly, the kangaroo.

It was some time towards the end of 1956 that I broke my Marius Eriksen skis. The snow had started to disappear from the runs at the top of Mt Franklin, so the more ardent club members drove further along the Brindabella range to the slopes of Little Mt Ginini where there was lots more snow. And a ski jump. Some time ago someone had built a jump over the road and carved a narrow approach leading to it. I had to try it. Unfortunately, in one attempt I made a bad landing and the front third or so of one of my skis broke off, hurtling through the air and finishing up in the snow gums some yards away. It took some time to locate. I carried the pieces back home and made enquiries in the university as to whether anyone could repair them. Someone advised me to ask around the physics department, and I eventually found a technician who offered to put the pieces together with the aid of some araldite. A two-part epoxy, called araldite, it had been invented just ten years before.

It was that year, too, that we had a narrow escape from disaster. We had decided to spend a week alone up at Mt Franklin lodge, and drive around to Little Mt Ginini for whatever snow remained. Late one afternoon we were reversing back along the road towards Mt Frankin when without warning our little Fiat station wagon suddenly slipped sideways on the ice, finishing with the two passenger-side wheels over the bank. What to do? First, we carefully extricated the boys through the rear door, Brett being just a few months old sleeping in a carry-cot, Gresham some twenty-one months older.

With them safely secure, I worked out a method of getting the car back on the road. Needless to say, there were no cell phones available at that time. And the nearest farm equipped with an ordinary landline must have been about 25 miles away. Being on a remote road, and midweek, we couldn't expect traffic to help. It was all up to me.

Here's what I did. I located two large boulders and, with the aid of a small folding spade I always carried in the trunk, embedded them in the soft mud just below the passenger-side tires. I used the boulders on which to rest the base of our tire jack. Then, one by one I would jack up the rear wheel and build a pyramid of smaller stones under the chassis next to the tire jack. Then I'd do the same for the front wheel. Finally, after several repetitions, I moved the tire jack around onto the driver's side and jacked up the car. It was now resting precariously on three points. Then, with Molly's help, we used all our concerted efforts to push the little car back onto the road, toppling the tire jack and two stone pyramids in doing so. Success! We had the Fiat back on the road. And in order to ensure there was no repetition of the sideways slide we collected dozens of twigs and small branches and placed them across the road to prevent slippage.

The next year, 1957, I was selected to represent our club in my first ski race. Held at Mt Kiandra, a one-time gold field in the Snowy Mountains, it was a daunting experience. The course was a giant slalom and by the time I started – somewhere towards the end of the field - navigating through the deep ruts in the slush was nearly impossible. I didn't make it for the second run. That was my introduction to ski racing. On a repaired pair of very old skis.

Towards the end of 1957, someone in the club set up a motor-bike powered rope tow to use on the lower slope of Little Mt Ginini.

Before that, one would ski down the top slope of Mt Franklin then climb one's way back up: a tedious, often painful, experience. That is what Molly and I had to do every year before 1958, the year of our departure for Sydney.

From then on, we seldom made the drive up to the ski chalet on Mt Franklin. Remember, from Part One, the problems that ensued from our life in Miranda: Molly's severe asthma; our retreat to Canberra in 1959; and our ultimate departure for Oxford at the end of 1960. There was little time to indulge in our passion for skiing, or even venturing into the Brindabellas.

Except for one occasion in the winter of 1960, just after I had heard of my post-doctorate grant to Oxford. I had heard of the newly constructed ski lift in Thredbo. A mile long, it had been built so as to facilitate the construction of the Kareela Hutte under the direction of an Austrian skier, Charles Anton. I had contacted Charles and booked a couple of nights at the 16-bed lodge. That was the first time we rode on a chairlift; the first time, too, I guided three-and-a-half-year-old Brett down the steepish slopes below. I did this in stages, teaching Brett to stand first with his skis across the slope, then to get into a snow-plough position, then to point them downhill and come to me who was waiting to catch him under his arms. We gradually increased the distance, until he was coming a full fifty yards or so, his velocity being such as to knock me flat on my back, sliding downhill with Brett pealing with laughter as he landed on my chest with his little grey plastic coat billowing out behind him. In that way we proceeded to the bottom of the lift, and so back to the top again. Once was enough.

Built in 1958, the Hutte is now being used as an outstanding

58

restaurant servicing the valley below.

3. To Oxford and Austria

I've already (in Part One) told the story of my year in Oxford. But not the part involving skiing.

In 1961 we made a week-long trip from Oxford to the little Austrian village of Lech. We obtained permission to park outside one of the hotels and stayed in our Doormobile campervan, with its lift-up lid and shoulder-level bunks for the boys. We enrolled the boys with a young ski instructor while we took instruction from a more experienced teacher. It was our first occasion skiing as a family.

4. Back to Canberra and Venturing to Mt Perisher

As already sketched in Part One, we returned to Canberra in 1962. By this time, the Canberra Alpine Club had built a new A-frame lodge in Mt Perisher, close to Ken Murrray's newly constructed Sun Deck lodge. And since Perisher Valley was replete with several chairlifts as well as T-bars and rope tows, it was natural for us to divert our attention from Mt Franklin to the newly constructed lodge in Perisher. True, it was much further to drive: through Cooma and Jindabyne, up to Smiggins Hole and – if snow conditions allowed – to the valley floor of Perisher itself. But many of our old friends from Canberra Alpine Club had transferred their allegiance to Perisher. And besides, the club had been joined by many new members with whom we became friends, a number of them being of European origin.

It was in Perisher that I first learned to ski reasonably fast. I had become friends with a young German-born ski instructor named Billy Ditmar, reputedly an ex German Junior ski champion. He would lead me; I would follow as close behind as I could, imitating his moves.

In the summer of 1962 he and I decided to participate in what was known as the mid-summer races at Mt Townsend, near the summit of Mt Kosciusko, Australia's highest peak. Getting there entailed many miles of driving from Perisher until one parked within view of Mt Townsend, then hiking miles across the tundra to the top of what was known as "the South America Drift" (so named for its distinctive shape). The meeting attracted ski racers from all over eastern Australia. Billy and I had waxed our skis appropriately for the melting conditions. He came first; I finished about three seconds behind, in fifth place. That was my first real success in ski racing.

Billy and I competed, too, in various quasi-gymnastic events at the Sun Deck on Saturday nights: leaning back and dancing under the limbo stick. Billy usually came first; I usually came second. Around 20 inches was our best performance. Meantime, Molly would spend the evening looking after the boys and socializing with friends back at the lodge.

Back to Billy. He, I am told, stayed in Perisher until 1970, then went to Aspen. I stayed in Perisher until the end of 1963, then went to New Zealand.

Another acquaintance of mine in those days was a young Austrian named Karl. One afternoon, late, we went on a training run together. On skis, up the valley under the col bridging Mt Perisher to its closest neighbour. We were just about to exit the valley when we noted a dark spot at the bottom of the slope. We had done the same route the previous evening and not noticed it. Together we decided to investigate. Just as well. There, lying inert on the snow, was a young girl who had apparently slipped down from the col on her skis and become unconscious. Karl and I picked her up and carried her, in turns, a mile or so to the nearest ski lodge where we left her to the tender mercies of the occupants. Karl and the young lass eventually entered into a relationship which ended sadly when she was found stealing from other members in the club. Invisible ink which turned red on contact with the human skin did the trick.

By then, I had learned to ski on cross-country skis. Fairly well, in fact. In 1962, I was nominated to set the course for the Australian cross-country championships in Perisher valley. I was secretary of the ACT (Australian Capital Territory) at the time. With the help of Swiss-French ski instructor, Jean Claude Ecuyer (head of the Perisher Ski School), we set a track of approximately 15 miles, intending to mark it with flags the next day. Unfortunately, the next afternoon a snow storm blew in obliterating our tracks and leaving us stranded and looking for shelter. We were in the process of digging a snow cave with the help of our ski tails, when Jean recognized a stand of snow gums as being (or being like) those behind a familiar hotel: The Man From Snowy River. We investigated. And he was correct. We were saved from a night or two of freezing cold. The race was postponed until the following weekend. Jean was to die a couple of years later when he drowned while fishing below a dam. Someone had misadvisedly chosen to release a flood of water from the dam above.

That year I met Richard Sykes. Fresh from doing a PhD at

Cambridge, he had been appointed as a Research Fellow in Philosophy at ANU. He had been introduced to me as an intrepid mountain climber, having neared the summit of Mt Masherbrun in the Himalayas before being forced to descend because of the death from high altitude pneumonia of one of his climbing party. He wasn't a skier when we met. But I soon taught him to ski modestly well; well enough to race in the New South Wales giant slalom down Perisher Mountain.

In 1963, I was training Richard on a sunny afternoon in Perisher when he announced his intent of walking back to Canberra cross country. He explained that he had come equipped to do so. Hence the heavy pack that he had carried down in the back of my VW Kombi bus. I thought he was crazy, especially when he invited me to join him. Molly, he explained, could drive the boys back to Canberra. He couldn't be talked out of his plan. For himself, that is. I certainly couldn't be talked into it. How would he find his way? He had a compass, he replied. And besides, in the clear weather we were enjoying he had a clear vision of the Brindabella Ranges. He'd be able to find his way across the myriad of streams and rivers that intervened. How long did he expect to take? He was confident he'd be back in Canberra by Thursday afternoon. If not, I was authorized to call out a search party.

Thursday came and went. No sign of Richard. The weather had changed on Wednesday. Low cloud hid the mountains. I made phone calls to club members seeking to recruit them to join me on Friday morning about 10:00 am. Three offered to join me. A sleepless night ensued. Then about 7:30 am Richard phoned. He had walked through a snow storm all night and had just staggered into a farm house somewhere below Piccadilly Circus. I called the search party off and drove out to pick up Richard. Had I remembered, he asked me, that we'd both been invited to a party on Saturday night out at the Royal Military College at Duntroon? I had remembered but presumed he wouldn't be in shape to attend. I picked him up the next night. Then followed an extraordinary feat of strength.

He challenged me to a competition of "Samson's chair" or sitting against the wall, out at Duntroon. It involved lowering one's back against a wall until you form a right angle at your hips and knees with your feet flat on the ground. Google recommends that one perform this exercise for about 20 seconds at a time, a minute at maximum if one is very fit. I did it for an hour and 15 minutes! Not to be outdone, Richard held that position for an extra two minutes! All to the applause of the military recruits who were doing the counting.

At the time we thought we must surely have broken the then-extant world record. Maybe. No one was keeping such records at the time. Google now tells me that the longest static wall sit was set on 20 December 2008 by a Vietnamese gymnast named Dr. Thienna Ho! She timed out at 11 hours 51 minutes and 14 seconds. Phenomenal! As you can find for yourself if you try doing it for as little as 5 minutes.

In 1963, I won the Canberra Alpine Club ski racing downhill championship. At the ensuing banquet, I was handed a huge silver cup brimful of champagne. I was set the task of taking a sip then passing the cup to banquet members to sip in their turn. Then I had to repeat to the cheers of all those present. I had nearly completed the rounds of 80 or so, with the cup being filled repeatedly with fresh bottles of champagne. By then I felt dizzy and had to excuse myself to go to the bathroom. Half an hour or so later Richard found me passed out on the floor of a men's cubicle. He had climbed over the wall, unlocked the door, and carried me out. Then he drove me home, unconscious. That was the first time, and the last, I allowed myself to get so drunk.

Shortly after winning the club championship I was approached by my Polish friend, Jan Gdowski, who said the time had come for me to decide between downhill and cross-country skiing. I could, of course, continue doing both, he said. But I was likely to do so indifferently. I thought about it for a week or two then decided to put most of my efforts into downhill skiing.

It was a timely decision because soon after we made the move to New Zealand where the terrain in the ski areas was not as suitable for cross-country skiing as it was in Australia.

5. THE MOVE BACK TO NEW ZEALAND AND MT RUAPEHU

The oldest, largest, and most prominent ski club in NZ was Ruapehu Ski Club (RSC). By the end of summer 1964 it had three huts: the Lodge sleeping sixty-seven; the Hut sleeping thirty-two; and the Chalet sleeping another thirty-two. The first two were located at the top of the first chairlift; the third near the bottom of the mountain Bruce Road.

We were warmly welcomed as members, and contributed two or three work parties before the snow season commenced: a prerequisite for making bookings for the ski season. When the snow started falling, we made two or three weekend trips down from Auckland to get familiar with how the lodge operated.

Then it was off to the South Island and the ski town of Queenstown, in our new Holden Station Wagon accompanied by the boys. We had arranged with our dear friends from Canberra Alpine Club, Lance and Stuart Burfield, to meet us in Queenstown when they flew over from Australia.

On meeting them, we first asked about their boys. They had two: both skiing friends of our boys, and about the same age. They were staying with Pat and his wife, mutual friends from the Canberra Alpine Club.

Then it was their turn to ask us a question: Had we heard about George, George Haynod, that is? The Hungarian who had taught me to ski? No, we hadn't.

Then they told us the story. A group of ten students from the ANU had driven into the lodge at Mt Franklin then been trapped there by a heavy snow fall. Even snow ploughs couldn't get through. The students had been missing for a week when some members of the club volunteered to rescue them. On skis. George led the group of rescuers that eventually led them out. It must have been a highly stressful trip. Two nights after returning home, George was heard by Loretta, his wife, going into the kitchen, mixing up an indigestion medicine, then collapsing on to the floor. He died about ten minutes later, from a ruptured stomach ulcer.

That was only a week or so before the Burfields arrived. No wonder no one had told us. Canberra Alpine Club members were still in shock.

Back to our visitors, the Burfields. We had rented someone's

65

home in Queenstown for two weeks. Each day Lance and I would fit into our ski boots and run up and down the seventy or so concrete stairs that led to our little house. Just to keep fit, we told ourselves. Then it was dressing in our ski gear, loading skis on to the roof rack, and off up the mountain sometimes pausing to help push a bus around a corner. The girls, Molly and Stuart, would go off skiing together; Lance and I, usually, by ourselves; and the boys Gresham and Brett, choosing whomsoever they wanted to join. We'd arranged to meet at the bottom of the first chairlift at midday.

One day, near the end of the first week, Lance didn't turn up at the appointed time. We waited for ten minutes or so before his wife Stuart began to get worried. Lance is usually so prompt, she explained. He may have broken a leg, or something. Would I go back up the chairlift to look for him? Gresham and Brett volunteered to join me.

Gresham and Brett and I were at one of the highest points on the lift, about 15 or 20 feet, when I saw someone being attended to by the ski patrol, off to my right. Judging by his distinctive ski boots, it was Lance. Then I saw the ski patrol pulling a blanket over Lance's face. I told the boys to secure themselves firmly in the lift.

Then I jumped. The snow was harder than I had estimated and I hurt my right elbow when I landed. I skied over to the scene I'd just witnessed and asked the patrollers what had happened. A woman ski racer whom I knew answered for them. She had been skiing behind Lance when he suddenly made a gurgling sound and toppled to the ground. The patrollers explained that they'd tried resuscitating techniques, without success. There was clearly nothing I could do. I waited for the boys to join me then skied down to the bottom of the lift with the news. It was one of the hardest things I've ever had to do: to tell a woman that her husband, the father of her two boys, was dead.

That afternoon, Stuart undertook the task of alerting our Australian friend, Pat Edmonds, with whom her boys were staying, about what had happened. Then followed various negotiations about the funeral, etc. I won't go into the details. Suffice it to say that we made arrangements to drive Stuart back to Auckland from where she took a flight back to Sydney and then back to her home in Port Kembla.

Molly and I were in shock. That was the third of our best friends to die. First my philosopher friend, Bruce Benjamin. Second, my French-polisher friend, Hungarian George Haynod. Third, my engineer friend, Lance Burfield. All three were aged about thirty-eight years. Less than forty anyway.

During the six or so years we were back in New Zealand, we treated Mt Ruapehu as a sort of home away from home. RSC had two huts we often used: the Lodge, up on hut flat, and the Chalet, just above the bottom of Bruce Road. And there was a third ski hut we had joined: named Ski Racer's Club, it was located about a third of the way up the first chairlift. We had made good friends in each and chose our destination according to the season, and the weather.

At Ski Racer's Club, we became particularly good friends with the president, Stan Blakely and his wife Sally. Then, too, there was Dr Murray Laird, as one of the two Vice-Presidents. I became the second VP.

Stan was particularly prominent as manager of the NZ Olympic ski team. And robust. He had been in the NZ Royal Navy in his younger years and was their wrestling champion. He enjoyed nothing more than being challenged to a tussle with one (or more) of the young "bucks" in the club. And flattening them.

Being members of two clubs at once gave us the privilege of extending our accommodation allowance in school holidays to a total of three weeks. And getting to know some of the North Island's best aspiring young racers.

During my sabbatical from Auckland University from August 1967 to May 1968, Molly and I had called in on some dear friends in London, Merle and Neil Thornton. We'd first met them in Canberra when I was doing my doctorate in Philosophy and Neil was studying for his doctorate in Political Science as well. Having failed to obtain his PhD in Canberra, he tried again in London. Success didn't look too promising as they had two young children on their hands, Harold and Sigrid, aged in each case about a year younger than our two boys. We persuaded Neil and Merle that they'd improve their chances of success if they were to send their children to stay with us in Auckland once we got back. Eventually they agreed and sent Harold and Sigrid back to us in the company of their grandparents.

It proved a wonderful success. In the nine or ten months that Sigrid and Harold were with us there wasn't a moment of friction between them and our two boys. Not that I can remember, anyway. Nor was there a murmur of protest from any of them about the hikes we took them on around the Ruapehu area. Not even the lengthy ones such as the five or six-hour trek from the Ketatahi Hut across the Rangipo Desert to the Ohinepango Springs, part of the Tongariro Alpine Crossing. These are all part of the Tongariro

National Park, the first place in the world to receive cultural World Heritage Status.

We have stayed in touch with the Thornton family ever since then and have followed Sigrid's outstanding acting career in such films as *The Man From Snowy River* (in which she co-starred with Kirk Douglas) with admiration and affection.

6. OUR MOVE TO CANADA

Skiing had been our passion ever since we took it up in Mt Franklin. We'd continued in Perisher, and at Ruapehu. Now it was time for a skier's paradise: Vancouver and Whistler.

In our first year there, we concentrated on getting settled. Then in what was left of the northern winter we tried skiing the local mountains, Grouse and Seymour, with only an occasional visit to Whistler.

Then, when we became most enamoured of Whistler, we joined the Tyrol Ski Club. As the name betokens, most of its members were of Central European origin. Many of them became very close friends. And many of them joined us in a new pursuit: sailing.

Although I didn't know it at the time I accepted Simon Fraser University's offer, one of the incentives they offered to the recruitment of senior academics was two years free of income tax. Had we arrived in Vancouver a few days later, we'd have been able to benefit to the tune of the full two years. But we didn't know that precise condition. So those few days that were spent in late December 1969 forfeited a whole year of tax benefit. Even so we benefited by a full year's tax write-off. And that made it possible for us to buy *Kia Ora*, a 26-foot sailboat that had been owned by some ex-kiwis. We had never been able to afford such luxury in our six years in New Zealand. Neither had we done any sailing. Not to worry. A day of sailing in a stiff breeze in nearby Howe Sound was enough to teach us the basics. And before long we were inviting our newly made friends to join us.

So it is that we started venturing around the coastline of the Strait of Georgia: a vast stretch of water that separated the British Columbia mainland from Vancouver Island. What particularly caught our attention was the group of islands to the north of the strait, including the area known as Desolation Sound and adjacent waters. We so fell in love with this area that, after two summers of sailing up there, we decided to sell the sailboat and buy a piece of land. That was in 1971, at the end of our second year of sailing.

There was a piece of land, partially forested, at the south entrance of an inlet running south of Desolation Sound known as Theodosia Inlet. It was nearly 40 acres in area and had a frontage on Theodosia Inlet of just over a quarter of a mile. The owner was asking $40,000. Too much for me alone. But if I could talk someone into sharing it with me, it would be within my scope. One of our Tyrol friends, Mark and Robyn Palliardia, flirted with the idea for a few weeks, then concluded that it was too far north of Vancouver where they, like we, lived. Getting there, via two-hour long ferry trips plus a six-and-a-half-mile boat trip from the end of the road at Okeover wharf took about six and a half hours.

Eventually I approached the Vice-President of SFU, Brian Wilson, to join me. He balked at the price. I argued him into making a firm offer of $30,000. Our offer was accepted!

7. Building at Theodosia

Brian and I agreed to build separate structures about a hundred yards apart: he a geodesic dome; I a log cabin built largely from trees I intended to fell from the property.

Brian's dome came in a kit-set and was quickly erected on a circular platform I had built for him in anticipation. All that remained for Brian to do was to adjust the pivot points by ensuring that they were symmetrical and sheathe the plywood with a suitable covering. For Brian, that task could be postponed. Going fishing took priority. Meanwhile a huge sheet of plastic would suffice to keep out wind and rain. It served that purpose for most of the winter; then had to be replaced by another. By that time the whole geodesic dome had warped irredeemably.

Eventually, after spending several summers up at Theodosia, Brian resigned his post at Simon Fraser University and accepted the position of Vice-Chancellor at the University of Queensland in Brisbane, leaving it to me to undertake the tasks that should have been performed at the beginning: putting in windows and sheathing the whole dome with asphalt tiles. All this was in order to stop the structure from rotting and making it suitable for occupation by a caretaker to look after the property in my absence.

So much for Brian's dome. When he went off to Australia, I bought out his share for an agreed price and made my own decisions without need for consultation with a partner. I had picked a building site on the edge of the flat area that comprised most of

71

the property. Reason? That provided us with a great view of Theodosia Inlet, filtered through immature trees that had been left standing by the previous owner.

During our first summer at Theodosia, 1972, I focussed on one thing only: felling trees that would be suitable for constructing a log cabin, and peeling off the bark. Some were cedars, some were firs, and some were hemlocks. One thing only was foremost in my mind: that each had to be about 10 inches in diameter. I had an old chain saw for the purpose and followed the instructions of logger friends from further up the inlet about how to fell a tree of 40 or 50 feet without having it land on me or fall on another tree. I learned, in fact, to have a tree fall on a predetermined spot, with a margin of error of a foot or two.

Where did we live during that first summer? Our acreage already had a little cedar-shake hut on it. We never did learn the history of its construction. Suffice it to say that it was about 10 foot wide by 12 foot long with a window at one end, a door at the other, and four bunks. Heating was supplied by a primitive woodstove.

8. CONFRONTATION WITH A BLACK BEAR

In preparation for spending our first summer in this little hut at Theodosia, we spent a weekend or so carrying boatloads of equipment, including an ample supply of food up to the hut. We had purchased a powerboat with a 120hp Evinrude motor and Auxiliary 6hp to carry us from the end of the nearest road at Okeover Inlet up the six miles of Lancelot Inlet to the entrance to Theodosia. And as a final touch, we brought more stores with us to start the summer.

We carried these fresh stores up the little path leading from the shore to the hut and covered them with a large tarpaulin.

Then came time to move our stuff from under the tarpaulin and put it into storage in the hut. I opened the padlock and reacted with shock and dismay. The scene that greeted me was of utter carnage. A bear had broken through the window, shattering broken glass into a dark, sticky, gooey substance all over the floor and spreading about 10 inches up the walls. Ants were over everything.

The only solution was to shovel it up, drill some holes through the floor, in anticipation of draining the residue, and heating water on the wood stove to dissolve the goo. This took hours. By the time we had finished, it was nearly midnight. We cleaned the bunks enough for us to prepare for sleep. But sleep didn't come easily. Not only did ants continue to drop on us, but our big dog, Rolf, (half boxer, half Alsatian) whom we'd brought over from NZ kept making growling noises as if to warn away a menacing animal. Not much sleep!

Next morning a quick inspection of the tarpaulin showed that many of its contents had been carried away. So Rolf's growls had not deterred the bear sufficiently. And it was time for us to replenish our stores by making a quick visit to the store at the little fishing village of Lund. We left Rolf to guard what remained and motored down the inlet to the wharf at Okeover, then took our Jeep Wagoneer through to the little village of Lund.

There we were greeted by the harbour master, Bob Wade, who invited us in for a quick lunch. I was in the process of telling him the saga and of how we had left Rolf to guard our remaining goods, when Bob interrupted with the caution, "Bears aren't afraid of dogs, even big ones like Rolf." Taking Bob at his word, we hurried back to the Okeover wharf, jumped in the boat and powered our way back up the inlet. No sooner did we enter our bay than the sound of an angry dog greeted our ears. The bear was back. Leaving Molly and the boys to anchor the boat, I jumped off into the shallow water and raced up the slope towards the hut. Quite evidently the bear had been at the tarpaulin again, despite Rolf's attempts to warn him off. Besides, a large paper sack of dog food had been torn off the branch to which I'd tied it. It had been torn open and was covered with bear slobber. No wonder Rolf was sounding so agitated!

We rescued what was remaining under the tarpaulin, and put some of it into the old refrigerator we had brought with us in one of our earlier trips, and left standing outside the cabin door. That night, like the previous one, was disturbed by sounds of the bear and sounds of a growling Rolf whom we'd left outside to perform guard duty.

Eventually, as the first glow of morning light illuminated the distant mountains, I opened the door to see what was going on. Rolf shot between my legs and cowered at the far end of the hut. I looked to the right. And there was a huge black bear (about 380 lbs according to the RCMP who subsequently measured it) making fruitless efforts to get into the fridge.

Following Bob Wade's advice, I had already purchased a 308 rifle with soft-nosed ammunition. It was hanging on the wall, waiting for just such an occasion as this.

"Give me my rifle, please," I called out to Brett. The bear had taken refuge behind a clump of fern from which he was watching me closely. I took aim but forgot to work the bolt. Nothing happened, of course, except that the bear, on hearing the sound, immediately ran towards and over a heap of cedar logs. I tried firing again. And missed.

It was my turn to head for the logs from which I caught sight of the bear running down an old logging road. Another shot. It obviously hit him because he tumbled over in an area surrounded closely by regrowth, mainly of young alder trees.

I followed until I saw splashes of blood on the clay. Then I stopped. The heavy breathing of a wounded bear came from all directions. I couldn't tell where. Backing out with rifle at the ready, I tried to calm my beating heart, then listened even more carefully. Finally, I thought I could hear a splashing sound. Ah-ha, I thought. He's trying to cool his wounds in a pool close by the old logging road. Warily, I waded through the blackberry bushes that surrounded the pool. Eventually I saw something moving among the black stumps that filled the pond. It was the bear's head. Aiming carefully this time, I fired. The bullet hit him in the centre of his head.

Time to retreat. "Bring me my sand-shoes," I called to Brett. I needed some protection from the blackberries. After all, since I first caught sight of the bear, I'd been in bare feet. And stark naked. I needed protection from the prickles.

When Brett arrived with a pair of sandshoes and a pair of shorts for me, we waded into the pool and eventually got hold of the bear's carcass and pulled him part way out. Part way only, note. He was too heavy to carry further. We decided to go back to the little hut and ponder the situation.

Meantime, Molly, upon hearing the shots and communicating with us about subsequent proceedings, had lit the stove and prepared breakfast. It was very welcome.

Our plan was this. We'd try tying his feet together, then placing a robust pole between them and see if we could carry him that way down to the edge of the inlet from which we would put him in a boat and transport him down to the Okeover wharf where there was a hoist that we could use to put him in Jeep and take him into Powell River for butchering.

Problems arose at the first stage. Our attempts at carrying him proved abortive. His body swung from side to side threatening to unbalance us both.

Solution? Make him lighter by disembowelling him and burying the stomach, etc. But even that didn't suffice. Taking recourse to the fact that we had a heavy-duty wheelbarrow, we put him in. And with one of us pulling on a rope and the other lifting the handles, we managed to get him down to the shore. There we managed to roll him into my partner Brian's 14-foot red plastic canoe that we towed down the inlet.

All went smoothly until about a mile from our destination. Then we hit a large wave generated by a passing boat. The weight of the bear broke the canoe in half and the bear's carcass started to disappear down the gap. Wheeling our motorboat around and manoeuvring it alongside the canoe, I managed to seize all that remained visible of the bear: one of its hind legs. Then with a twisting movement I managed to make its other hind leg emerge. Then, together, Brett and I hauled the whole carcass over the bear's body over the side of our boat until its head came to rest in a bucket containing its heart and liver. Gross, but strangely amusing.

The rest of the trip was straightforward enough. We stopped

76

outside the shop of a butcher with whom I'd had past dealings and asked if he would cut up the bear for us. Do you have a licence, he asked? No? Then I suggest you obtain one from the RCMP, he said.

A member of the RCMP said he'd want to see the bear for himself in order to corroborate my story. The fact that I was a comparatively recent immigrant from NZ led plausibility to my tale. A stern lecture about the need for bear licences and for registering my gun was all that he subjected me to. Then back to the butcher who lent Brett and me sharp knives for the purpose of skinning the bear and left us to it after advising us how to proceed. An hour or so afterwards, he trimmed the pieces for us and wrapped them up for freezing. We could pick them up when we returned to Vancouver, he said.

End of the bear story! Except to add that the bear meat didn't taste that good. Not surprising! Among other things, the bear had eaten (or drunk) quite a lot of gasoline that we had left in storage in our little cedar-shake hut.

"Bear's revenge" we called it.

I paid for the killing in another way, too. I undertook to erect a raised foundation for Brian's geodesic dome in reparation for sinking his canoe.

All that occurred in our first summer at Theodosia.

9. PLANNING AND CONSTRUCTING OUR OCTAGONAL LOG CABIN

In our second summer, 1973, we built the first storey of our log cabin. But first we had to decide on a design. I spent winter evenings at the Tyrol Ski Club pondering the possibilities. Foremost in my thinking was the idea of maximizing the square area given that the perimeter would have to be determined by logs. I thought about the geometrical fact that the maximum area for a given perimeter would be secured by a circle. But how could I construct a circle from logs? Most log cabins with which I was familiar took the shape of squares. But standard ways of constructing a square with the 24-foot logs I had at my disposal would yield - once the usual notched overlap was allowed for - a square of 20x20 i.e. 400 square feet. Not good enough for all that hard work. Eventually, I reasoned that I could obtain a floor area of optimal size if made an octagon. This would be possible if I cut the 24-foot logs in half then found a way of effectively butting the ends together at each apex of the octagon.

I worked out a way of doing just that.

Simply described it consisted of erecting a log pole in each corner of the octagon, nailing 2x8 inch cedar boards vertically at the appropriate angle, and cutting each end of the horizontal logs that would form the walls so that they constituted a tongue to be nailed on to the vertical 2x8's.

First, I had to erect poles for the foundation of the whole structure. Nine sufficed for my plan to work: eight for the corners and one for a centre pole, each put on a sturdy concrete foundation. For the centre pole I located a huge gnarly piece of yellow cedar that would support heavy duty 6x12 inch beams for the ceiling. More 6x12 inch cedar beams for the floor were put into appropriate size notches at the top of each of the corners. In effect, I designed a spiderweb for the ground floor of the cabin to be. Ditto for the ceiling.

I'll skip the rest of the procedure. Suffice it to say that both the

78

floor and the ceiling were laid by Molly and Gresham using red cedar tongue and groove boards. Once done, for each of the eight sectors of the cabin, they constituted quite an elegant sight.

Where did the beams, floorboards, and other milled timber come from? Bob Wade, as well as being harbour master at the fishing village of Lund, owned and operated a little cedar mill. He supplied to order. And would deliver the product down to the Okeover wharf. It was up to me to pick it up there and transport it on my boat or on a huge log float borrowed from one of the logging camps located about three miles further up Theodosia Inlet. There were exceptions, of course. When it came to constructing a set of stair-treads to go upstairs, I used my chainsaw to cut them from the remains of the yellow cedar.

I devised a secret mechanism to lock the robust front door to keep out intruders. It worked well.

At the end of the summer semester we covered the whole structure with a pile of overlapping newspapers and a huge piece of plastic on top. It withstood the winter rain and snow without a leak.

When we came back for the next summer period, 1974, we got to work on constructing the second storey in a different manner from the first: eight 12-foot poles in a circle in the centre and eight 6-foot poles at the apex of the octagon, each centre pole being connected with the outside one by means of a 24-foot beam slotted into a notch cut with my chain saw. These beams, of course, were too heavy to lift into place. So I rigged up a guy rope and used an electric winch to hoist them into place. The winch was attached to the front of my Jeep Wagoneer that I'd towed into place on the big float borrowed, as usual, from one of the logging camps up the inlet. The float also carried a couple of steers that I'd brought in to keep the grass down and eventually to be slaughtered for their meat.

The centre circle of poles, at their tops, formed an octagon to support a huge piece of tempered glass. Other pieces of tempered glass formed windows for the upstairs bedrooms. All pieces of tempered glass were slightly warped, including those for the ground floor. So, I obtained them all from a manufacturer for nothing.

The whole of the roof was made waterproof by covering it with roles of asphalt. This was done with the help of my brother Neville and his wife Beryl who were visiting us from New Zealand.

By then we had installed a beautiful wood-burning stove. I say "beautiful" because it had been manufactured somewhere in the US using nickel, instead of chrome, as trim. It was dated 1896. The story of how we came to acquire it would take too long to tell. Suffice it to say that we found it in an old shed owned by one of the logging bosses, Nick Malenko. "Full of junk," Nick said. "Throw it into the salt-chuck." But when he heard of our intent, he let us have the stove for nothing. And after a week of grinding and polishing to get rid of the rust, Brett and I were able to move it into the kitchen and put it into use. It made an elegant addition to the gas stove we put in next to it.

We also installed a gas refrigerator and gas lighting on each of the downstairs corner poles. That entailed bringing in a 45 kg gas cylinder that we stored outside.

That brings up another story. I had recognized the need for a supply of electricity and purchased a 4.5kilowatt diesel generator. Gresham, Brett, and I erected a small shed deep in the forest so as to keep it relatively quiet. We built a small sled on which to carry it from the beach and hauled it into place using the Jeep. By then it was pitch black dark. Suddenly we were startled by the bloodcurdling scream of a nearby cougar. Leaving our tools in place, we hastened back to the Jeep and backed in out the narrow path through the trees to the new octagonal cabin. We left the matter of installing a big cable connection between the generator and the cabin until the next morning.

So that's how Brett and I managed to use an electric drill to polish the woodstove.

As for cougars, they abounded in our area. This was evident from the deep scratches they left on trees; and from the fact that the following year, my caretaker for the winter heard a thump as he was taking a bath and looked up to see a cougar staring down at him through the skylight. Just as well the skylight was made of thick tempered glass!

In the summer of 1975 I put the finishing touches to the cabin by building a lean-to extension containing a flush toilet, bath, and sauna. The flush toilet, of course, entailed digging a deep cedar-lined sump. The bath entailed putting in a gas heater for hot water. The sauna entailed installing a wood-burning heater and chimney. The whole bathroom area was illuminated during daylight hours by aforementioned skylight, and at night by another gas burning light.

Meantime, we had noted that the beach area had become covered by young oysters. Not only for our own beach but for the beaches opposite in what was designated as part of the Desolation Sound Marine Park. This motivated me to apply for an oyster-harvesting licence and apply for permission to build an oyster packing plant.

Right at the beginning of 1972, we had found a supply of fresh water flowing into the inlet, dug a little dam which we lined with plastic, and put in a ¾ inch plastic pipe to supply our drinking needs. The water pressure was about 76 pounds per square inch. Subsequently, we put in a holding tank at the side of the cabin, and put an extension of the water pipe down the hill to the packing plant.

It then occurred to me that the water pressure was adequate to power a small Pelton wheel, and thereby run an electric cable back up to the cabin, replacing the need for gas powered lights and allowing for a set of batteries for electricity storage. That, in turn, allowed me to install a radiotelephone to communicate with the outside world and power other electric devices such as a CD player and loud speakers. The Pelton wheel was set up to run all the time so that the set of storage batteries were dribble-fed to operate when needed.

My applications for oyster harvesting and the packing plant were successful. It remained for me to find a means of transporting the oysters, as well as the underlying clams, down to Vancouver. In this, too, I was successful there by providing income for the caretakers who did the harvesting of both oysters and clams.

10. MOVING FROM WEST VANCOUVER TO WHISTLER

Sometime in 1977 we sold the house in West Vancouver and built a 4-storey house at Whistler. The Whistler house, like the octagonal cabin at Theodosia, was built to my design. It was superbly located with uninterrupted views of Whistler Mountain and easy access both from one of the ski runs leading down from the main run down the mountain and easy exit from the road in front of the cabin down to the bottom of the main chairlift (a gondola).

At that time, Blackcomb Mountain had not yet been developed. And the village, which now forms the heart of "Whistler" was still a wasteland used for dumping rubbish and hence inhabited mainly by black bears. One could ski down one of the runs to be picked up infrequently by a bus. But otherwise one had to rely on private transport.

Our house was begun in early 1977, and constructed partly by someone who was to become a close friend: Peter Lazier. He was a very interesting guy. He had a law degree from Ontario but had abandoned practise of the law to undertake more outdoor pursuits such as cycling from Ontario to the east coast of Canada, repeating the feat by kayaking across most of Canada, and using his motorbike to travel cross-country across northern British Columbia.

At one point, he gave me a ride on his new motorbike from Vancouver to Whistler. It was hair-raising to say the least. I was in pillion position, hanging on to Pete as he rode at enormous speed up the tightly curved "highway" along Howe Sound and then up the even more tightly curved road from Squamish to Whistler. It was with a suppressed breath of relief that we finally stopped at the house.

Pete co-operated with another skiing friend of mine, Brian Allen, in designing and building a set of benches and cupboards to match out of fir timber facing the mountain on the third floor. Above this was a fourth floor containing a bedroom and study. Below was a small self-contained flat that we rented to Brett and his girlfriend of the time, Beth. Plus, a sloping glass pottery studio built in

83

anticipation of Molly using it to pursue her ambitions in the field of potting. Molly never got around to using it, or the potter's wheel and tons of clay I had purchased for her.

On the ground floor was an area in which we made provision for parking our vehicle. And a large wood-burning fireplace plumbed in such a way as to heat water for the two cylinders up on the third floor.

As for "our" bedroom, it was constructed on the third floor with superb views of the mountain and the forest below.

11. GOING OUR SEPARATE WAYS

By the time if came for me to take a sabbatical leave, in September 1977, my relationship with Molly had deteriorated to the point where we decided amicably to go our own separate ways. While we were still living in West Vancouver, Molly had begun taking pottery lessons at Capilano College in North Vancouver and decided to pursue them further at Goldsmith College of the University of London for a year. I encouraged her to the extent of financing her in her efforts. And I continued to do so for decades longer until we eventually, in the early 90s, proceeded to divorce each other.

During the whole of that time we kept on making efforts to accommodate each other's wishes to use the two properties we then possessed: the octagonal log cabin at Theodosia and a new 4-storey cabin at Whistler. My design for the new cabin in Whistler made provision for the lavish pottery studio to await her return from Goldsmiths College. Unfortunately, for reasons to do with her mother's death in New Zealand, she never used it.

We seldom saw each other in person, having found other "relationships" to enjoy. In my case, with several different women; in her case with many different women as well as men. Eventually, we tried to agree to terms for a legal separation.

Unfortunately, we got nowhere. Molly went to a female lawyer who was widely known as a "balls buster". The terms on which she insisted were so at variance with what I and my own legal adviser thought fair that negotiations broke down. Molly resumed living her favoured lifestyle of partying, going to nightclubs such as the Penthouse, and travelling around the province (e.g. to the Queen Charlottes) and repeatedly down to Washington where her latest male lover lived. We had almost no contact with each other, but I continued to pick up the bills. Her spending was not wildly irresponsible but was nevertheless costly.

It wasn't until Molly's Uncle and Aunt died leaving her a considerable inheritance that I tried again. This time her lawyer was a much more reasonable woman. I asked my lawyer if he would represent me. He said that, in his opinion, I could handle negotiations myself. I did so, to good effect. We finally agreed to a split of real property with Molly, who had no income other than her inheritances, taking the cabin at Whistler; and me, who had income from employment at SFU, taking Theodosia. I was relieved of the obligation to support her financially. Molly soon sold the cabin at Whistler, at considerable profit. I sold Theodosia in 1990 at a much lower price.

12. Purchasing and Flying a Lake Amphibian 200hp

Travelling to and from Vancouver to Theodosia by car and ferry was fairly expensive. And costly in terms of time: about 6-7 hours. It would be much more effective if I could learn to fly, buy a seaplane, and make the trip from the university up to Theodosia in about an hour or so.

In 1977, when I was forty-six years old, I resolved to learn how to fly. Getting to the Pitt Meadows airfield from the university took about 25 minutes at the most. There I learned to fly a Cessna. As part of qualifying for a Pilot's Licence I had to learn how to handle a spin. After some hesitation, I eventually mastered the skill and came to enjoy it. Gerry, my tutor, pronounced me qualified after about 20 hours of his tuition. I went for my licence and secured it at first attempt.

Now was the time to look for, and purchase, a seaplane of choice: a four-seater Lake Amphibian. I eventually found one: the first 200hp ever manufactured. It was located up in the interior, somewhere near Nelson. After fuelling up, and handing over the asking price of $45,000, we took off. My lesson in flying the amphibian consisted of several landings and take offs from both land and water. All went smoothly until we landed near the owner's residence where he disembarked. Then after listening to some cautionary reminders and refuelling, it was left to me to fly back to Pitt Meadows where I'd left my car. All went well, though I had to land on a small lake for the night because of lowering cloud levels. The denizens of the nearby town had seen me land and applauded my caution.

86

I used the plane not only for transport to and from Theodosia, but also to transport bags of seafood. I could take off from Pitt Meadows and land on the inlet at Theodosia, then taxi up the beach, wash my plane down with fresh water and tie it down on little grassy area next to the packing plant. Only seldom did I venture much from that pattern, although I well recall making trips up to lakes at Whistler and once ventured out over the western shores of Vancouver Island looking for a little village where Paula Swan and her Indian husband Joe David were living at the time.

Two or three years later, I had a rare call from Molly. She would like to join me on my next trip to Theodosia. I agreed and picked her up at a jetty on the Sechelt Inlet, about half way to Theodosia. It was then that I explained more fully than I had during our brief telephone call. The caretakers at that time had found that contents of the oyster trays they had in storage seemed to be getting rotten. They wanted me to advise what to do. About 6,000 lbs, it turned out. Apparently, my caretakers had taken advantage of an offer from some unlicensed oyster pickers to buy them cheaply. They thought I'd be pleased. But it turned out that they had over-packed the trays, putting in several layers of oysters as opposed to the single layers I'd advised in circumstances like these.

Result? I spent most of the night sorting out dead and dying oysters, trying to salvage the few remaining good ones.

I really wasn't in good condition to fly back to Vancouver. Making things worse, were the weather conditions: low overcast and drizzly. Then there was a problem with the mandatory registering of my flight plan. I tried to contact the airfield at Comox on Vancouver Island from the aircraft radio. But they couldn't hear me clearly. I tried to contact them with the radiotelephone back in the cabin. But low cloud and the intervening Bunster Mountain made that difficult too. I decided to take off and try again once I'd gained enough altitude. We flew down the inlet, climbed over the neck of land that separated the inlet from Powell Lake, and tried again. But static made our attempt fruitless.

It was my intent to land in the narrow piece of water separating Bunster Mountain from Goat Island. This was my usual practice, in order to wash off the saltwater, and I trimmed the plane up to make the usual landing. A problem then became clear. As we flew down the 30-odd mile long lake we were confronted by the fact that the water below perfectly matched the dark cloud above. We were, in effect, trying to make a landing on what pilots call "glassy water". Worse still was our loss of depth perception. I couldn't tell how far we were above the glassy water. I thought we had 20 feet or so to spare so pushed lightly on the yoke with the intent of pulling the yoke back to make the usual soft landing. But the water of the lake was closer than I thought.

And when I was expecting to be greeted by a soft "Sshh", I heard a loud "Bang" instead. No more sensations until I found myself skipping across the surface for about 90 feet calling to my wife "Molly," "Molly," with increasing urgency. Molly, it turned out, had been trapped under the fuselage of the sinking plane until she emerged with blood streaming down her face. There wasn't time to explain what had happened or why. Suffice it to say that the plane had broken just behind the cabin, and then flipped over, breaking the seat belts that tied us each in, ejecting me at about 50 kph, and injuring us both. Molly's injuries were less serious than mine: scalp injuries and a nasty cut on one of her legs. My injuries were worse:

torn back muscles, a broken ankle, and a hyper-extended left knee causing the ligament to tear right off the bone. No wonder I found it difficult to make my way to the sinking fuselage of the plane.

Well before I reached it Molly had popped up on the other side. We each put on the life jackets that fortuitously were floating within reach and made our way to the shore of Goat Island. I reached there first and had considerable difficulty crawling out of the freezing water and up the steep slope (about 45 degrees). Molly had chosen to swim on her back and had little difficulty climbing out. The ice had only recently thawed. After all, it was the 3 May 1983.

We had crashed at about 10:10 am to judge from Molly's watch that had stopped on immersion. I crawled up the slope as far as my injuries allowed and finally rested in a mossy hollow. At about 1 pm it started to rain. Molly busied herself with gathering bark to cover me when we heard the sound of a motorboat approaching from the direction of Powell River. It had three occupants: a woman who was piloting and two male occupants in the back, both with industrial first aid certificates. Molly managed to draw the woman's attention by waving her life jacket vigorously. The woman throttled back and used her radiotelephone to call the RCMP.

About half an hour later the police turned up in a floatplane and put Molly in to fly her to the Powell River dock where an ambulance was waiting to transport her to the Powell River hospital. Then they came back for me. By the time they reached me I was fading fast. The two guys with industrial first aid certificates had evaluated me and come to the conclusion that I had a broken back. They demanded that I be put in a stretcher. But the RCMP had forgotten to bring anything to tie me in. Following my suggestions, they used the motorboat to gain access to a little cabin about half a mile away, break in, and tear a blanket into strips for the purpose. They had some difficulty bridging the gap between the rocky shore and one of the floats. Had they dropped me, I would have gone down to about 360 feet below the surface. After all I was tied into a heavy metal stretcher; and that is the depth at which a salvage boat eventually located the wreckage of my plane. Thankfully, after a fumble or two by the helpers, I made it to the nearest float of the seaplane and followed Molly's route to the hospital.

Doctors there put me in the Emergency Ward on the grounds that I was suspected to have internal bleeding as well as a broken back. But they were wrong on both scores. A day or two later a local doctor suggested he might try operating on my left knee. I rejected his offer on the grounds of his non-expertise. He had never before operated on someone with an anterior cruciate ligament that had been torn off the bone and required stapling. Gresham agreed, having been told of my condition. He phoned the hospital at the University of British Columbia. They sent an air ambulance to pick us both up. Once at the University Hospital, I was operated on by an ex-NZ surgeon who usually worked for the Vancouver Canucks (ice hockey players). Molly needed no such services, having sustained only a badly gashed leg. Nonetheless they put us both in the same room for the duration of our stay. I was put in a plaster cast extending from just below the groin to near the toes of my left foot in order to cater for the repair of both my left knee and my broken left ankle.

13. RESUMING SKIING, 1984

On our release, we went to stay with our ex-neighbours, Allison and Peter Burnett, who had a heated swimming pool in which I was able eventually to exercise my leg. It took some months before my cast could be removed and my knee put in a leg brace, some months before I was able to resume skiing.

In fact, it was only in my third season of skiing, after the accident, that I suddenly found myself skiing without the support of my brace. And by then I had already taken part twice in the longest giant slalom race in the world: the "Peak to Valley" race involving something like 180 gates. In both cases I was racing as part of a team of four.

In the five years between then and the beginning of the 1989 ski season, I had gained confidence in skiing. I had joined Brett in his pursuit of so-called "Extreme Skiing": skiing down couloirs, jumping down cliffs, skiing fast through dense forests, etc., often in areas marked "FORBIDDEN". I didn't have the courage to join him in some of the more extreme of his ventures, but often dared where less venturesome skiers wouldn't feel comfortable. One example is the narrow chute down from the top of Blackcomb Mountain. An Australian ski instructor joined us in that venture. But his legs were shaking uncontrollably as he sideslipped his way down the narrowest part of the chute.

During that period, I occasionally took part in other "open" ski races; ones that were usually won by members of a race-training group called the "Masters". It wasn't until towards the end of the 1988 ski season that I was encouraged by Alfred (Freddie)

Zielberger to join them. Freddie was a fellow member of the Tyrol Ski Club and knew how fast I could ski. I just needed to have my technique polished by some experts, he argued. And having witnessed the likes of Freddie himself and Bob Switzer running the gates underneath me as I rode the lift to the top of the FIS Downhill course, I knew what he meant.

14. SELLING THEODOSIA, BUYING PINECREST IN 1990

By the end of 1989 it became obvious to me that I would do well to sell Theodosia and move to the Whistler area. I did so just in time to purchase a log cabin that had been moved from the waterfront in West Vancouver to the edge of Pinecrest Lake, a development located about 20 km south of Whistler Mountain. It was located in a gated community at the south end of the lake, with beautiful views to the north of the mountain range opposite Whistler Mountain. It took only about fifteen minutes to reach the base of the mountain.

During the eight or so years of my ownership, I made several modifications to the layout, including adding on a second bedroom and building a dining room extension over an extensive west-facing deck right next to a large hot tub. It was the proximity to the mountains that motivated me to make the move to Pinecrest. And the fact that it made the drive to SFU that much briefer. (I was still teaching at the University.) I had negotiated a teaching schedule of three days a week.

That left the other two days of the week for me to pursue my goal of ski racing in the early part of the morning, (up until 10:30 am or so) then retire to my new cabin for lecture preparation and research during the afternoon.

15. MOVING TO WHISTLER ITSELF (BRIEFLY)

In 1996, I married for a second time. Belinda was born in England but had moved to New Zealand in her early twenties. She was a widow by the time I met her on a trip to NZ. She had borne two children, Sarah and Timothy Lichtenstein, both of whom were good skiers.

Two years or so later, Belinda expressed the desire to move from Pinecrest to a suburb of Whistler itself. With some reluctance, I obliged.

I came to regret it when the marriage lasted only two more years. In 2000, while we were visiting NZ, Belinda declared, without real explanation, that our marriage was over. I was dismayed.

16. BACK TO NEW ZEALAND (IN 2000)

On due reflection, I decided that there was no way in which I could afford to stay in Canada. Reasons?

(a) There was no way in which I could return to the paradise of living on the lakeside on Pinecrest. I had sold that to one of my best friends, Randall Carpenter, and her husband, Jim, coach of the Canadian women's Ski Team. The only property within financial reach would be a relatively small apartment in Whistler itself.

(b) I had close family and friends back in NZ: including one of my sons, Gresham, who had returned two years earlier; one of my brothers, Neville, and his wife, Beryl and family; and close friends such as Robert Nola, Barry Holdaway and Wilton Willis, plus numerous ex-students from my time as Head of the Philosophy Department at Auckland back in the 60s.

(c) The exchange rate, at that time, meant that the income from my retirement would go much further when translated from Canadian superannuation to NZ dollars. This last reasoning proved to be illusory when the Canadian authorities wrote to me telling me that they had made a mistake in their calculations, arguing that I was entitled to only half, the other half being due to Molly. I did not dispute their calculations.

For reasons such as these, I made the choice of returning to NZ, where, in October 2000, I purchased a property in Omaha beach, about 80 km north of Auckland, and made plans for the design of a new beachside home. To the date of writing, June 2018, I have been there ever since.

The octagonal cabin completed, 1975

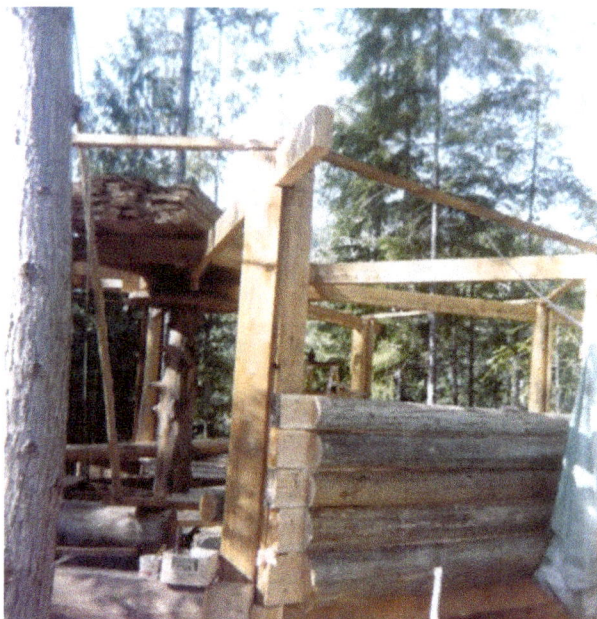

Above: Constructing the first floor, 1973

Below: Constructing the second floor, 1974

Above: Constructing the second floor, 1974

Below: Inside the living room

Above: Raymond in his Lake Amphibian visiting friends in a nearby inlet

Below: Bringing Jeep and cattle to the cabin in Theodosia Inlet

Aerial view of the completed cabin

THREAD 3: MY SUCCESSES IN SKI RACING

1. JOINING THE WHISTLER MASTERS GROUP

Prior to 1989, I had won - and won medals or trophies in - countless ski races of all genres (from Slalom and Giant Slalom to Downhill) in Australia, New Zealand, and Canada. But most of them were at the club level. And in preparation for none of them did I receive training by expert ski racers. My approach to each was relatively amateurish, being guided only by my own careful analysis of videos taken of younger World Cup ski racers in FIS events.

It should be noted that events held in New Zealand do not feature in the following summary because national titles in my home country were not decided, as in most other countries, by single events but by a set of results held across the two islands.

2. THE NEW SPEED EVENT OF SUPER G

It soon became apparent that racing without training was not good enough.

In 1983 a new discipline of ski racing was introduced by the FIS (International Ski Federation). A cross between Downhill and Giant Slalom it constitutes another "speed event" as compared to the "technical events" of Slalom and Giant Slalom. Given my aptitude for Downhill it appealed to me as a discipline that would suit me well.

But I did not know how to ski it.

About five years later, in 1988 (or thereabouts), I joined the Masters training group at Whistler, hoping to remedy my deficiencies. We had first-rate training from world-class coaches such as Jacques Morel, a one-time member of the French National Ski Team, plus various members or ex-members of the Canadian Ski Team, such as Gordie Brown and Glen Wurtele. Jacques was an expert in the technical discipline; Gordie and Glen were experts in the speed events. I owed much to all three, plus other coaches, such as Chris Kent.

3. Results of Good Training

By the end of my first year of race training (1988) I proved to be only a "hack" racer, as judged by my place in the Canadian Ski Championship. As I recall it, I placed only about fifth out of a field of about twenty racers in my group.

In my second year (1989) I did better: I placed first in the Canadian Combined Championship for my group.

4. FIS and Groups

It is time to explain what I mean by "group".

The Whistler Masters group was a local organization that was a member of the FIS. It provided rules for alpine ski racers aged thirty or more and categorized them into classes each spanning five years. For example, the class to which I belonged upon joining was group B6 spanning the ages 55-59. The next class was B7 spanning ages 60-64. And so on. It laid down rules governing FIS points, and ranked skiers in order of their points, the lowest starting first.

5. TRAINING FOR SUPER G

Unfortunately, the FIS MASTER organization did not recognize the discipline of Downhill, the fastest of the two speed events, for points purposes. I lamented this fact because I fancied my chances in Downhill as being better than those in the new discipline of Super G. (As the following summary shows).

In 1991, my rival and close friend, Bud White, and I decided to hire a renowned ski coach from Backcomb Mountain to teach us the fine art of crossblocking (for Slalom) and how best to race the much faster discipline of Super G.

Bud White was an interesting character. He was a world–renowned fighter pilot, having once held the world altitude record. And he was a good ski racer, too. We learned much about both disciplines. And from skiing together.

It showed in our FIS points in both events.

6. MY FIRST WORLD CHAMPIONSHIP PLACING: SILVER

It wasn't until my third year (1991) in Masters I decided to pit my skills against others at the world championship level.

I therefore ventured to race in an international FIS race. It was called the FIS Criterium Mondial (World Championship) and it was held in Winter Park, Colorado.

As I recall it both Bud and I registered for the Winter Park events and drove down together. I forget how Bud fared. But I do remember my results. They were all the more memorable because some six weeks before, I had injured myself badly while training for a downhill event on Whistler. I had fallen on an icy patch just after a steep section of the course and cracked my pelvis. A fellow Masters ski racer, who happened to be an orthopaedic surgeon, visited me and advised me against following through on my plans to race in Winter Park but counselling me to spend as much time as I could doing exercises in my hot tub at Pinecrest. I followed his advice about exercises but made the trip as planned.

I had modest success in both of the technical events, slalom and giant slalom failing to win a medal in either.

And in Super G, I had little prospect of much success. After all, because I lacked any FIS points, I was ranked 34th out of a field of 38 racers. I wasn't surprised to hear, before I started, that the first three places had already been settled, temporarily, by racers from Austria.

I wasn't to find out who won, who was second, or who was third, until I finished. It was then that I was told that I had upset the Austrian applecart by coming second, just 15 hundredths of a second behind the winner, Sepp Ortner. The other Austrians took my silver medal placing in good grace. Sepp showed his brilliance by also winning the other two races: Slalom, and Giant Slalom.

(It is worth noting in passing that the Criterium Mondial is held in North America only once every five years. And even then it alternates between the USA and Canada. Otherwise it is held somewhere in Europe.)

7. THREE GOLDS IN WORLD CHAMPIONSHIPS (SUPER G)

The silver medal I achieved in Super G at Winter Park, in 1991, proved not to be my best result ever in World Championships.

In the Super G held in Copper Mountain six years later, in 1997, I dismayed everyone (including myself) by winning. I owed my victory largely to my friend, the US coach Warren Witherell. He had told me much about the new developments in ski technology, about the new "shaped skis" and the chances of my failing to win anything again until I made the switch to short and shaped. I had already had this demonstrated for me in a recent GS race at Park City. There I had been soundly beaten into first place by three US racers who'd already made the transition. Through them I sought to find similar skis from their suppliers. But they'd all sold out. So they said.

So it wasn't until later in my five-week trip from Canada that I managed to find a supplier of what I was looking for. I was racing in Steamboat Springs, Colorado, when I found that a friend from Sun Valley, Idaho, was skiing on newly shaped Rossignol racing skis. She said she thought there was a similar pair still for sale back home. She phoned and checked and assured me her ski retailer had said he would hold the skis for me until I arrived next afternoon. Problems were: first, Sun Valley was at least five and a half hours away; second, I would have to change from the 210 cm Salomon skis I'd been given by my sponsors at the time to the much shorter 198 cm Rossignols. I decided to make the long drive back to Sun Valley, Idaho, intending to explain the switch from Salomon to Rossignol at a later date. I made the trip in just over five and a half hours and got to the ski retailer before 4 pm. The technician agreed to have my new Rossis mounted, waxed, and ready for me to ski the next morning.

I picked them up and went up the mountain with some of the local boys. They found my newly acquired skills amazing. I was digging "trenches" in the snow when I turned. I knew instantly that I'd made the right decision. I would have no difficulty selling my Salomons at a later date. After all they were World Cup stock, much in demand through the racing community.

Back to the race at Copper Mountain. My newly acquired Rossignol skis proved to be a wonderful success. As I say, I won the gold medal.

By this time, 1997, I had been appointed to the FIS Masters Committee. And a fellow member, the USA's Bob Bernard, was the first to greet me at the finish. "Ray," he said, "you have just won the World Championship." The field in my class (category) at that time numbered about 45-50 racers, about half of them being Europeans.

Next (in 2001) came the Super G event in Park City, Utah. Park City was one of my favourite venues. Again, I won, though I don't remember anything particularly memorable about the event, except being congratulated by the Head Coach at Park City, Bill Skinner, who had himself just won the World Championship for the same event for his class. I do remember, however, that he admitted to having found his Salomon skis too stiff and had handed them over to a young ski coach so as to "break them in."

And then came my victory in Abetone, Italy, in March 2002. It was an unexpected win. After all, the race was well and truly "out of season" for me from the southern hemisphere. And I was competing with someone, Sepp, who already had won gold medals in World

Championships on eleven occasions.

For the three weeks before competing in Abetone, I had been staying with Sepp Ortner and his wife Lotte in their village in the southern part of Austria, Bad Kleinkirchheim. During that period we had done some training at his home ski field, mainly in slalom and GS, and raced three or four times in local events held elsewhere in Austria, plus Germany and Switzerland. Each of us had victories to celebrate. By the time we left to drive down to Italy, I was getting into shape again.

After three weeks, Sepp and I drove in his VW Golf sedan, down to the Criterium Mondial in Abetone. We paused on the way in Venice, then drove on.

Sepp had persuaded me to race in the slalom. I did so and finished in 8th place. In Giant Slalom, I finished in the Bronze Medal position (3rd place).

But in Super G, I beat Sepp into first place by the slender margin of eight hundredths of a second.

The other racers in our group, mainly Austrians and Swiss, were very gracious with their congratulations at breakfast next morning. To us both. One by one they approached our table and shook our hands; sometimes even giving us both warm hugs. It was a very touching experience. I'd never been treated like this before.

Sepp and I never met again. But we have kept in touch by letters and photographs to this day.

8. Total Number of National and International Championships

It is worth noting that my best results, before I retired at the beginning of 2006, (at the age of seventy-five years) were mostly in the "speed events" of Downhill and Super G. I was never able to ski again. I tried training for the Canadian Downhill Championships at Silver Star in 2006 but had to stop on the way down the first run.

My retirement was occasioned by excruciating pain in my left knee. For the previous few years, I had made the pain bearable by having my left knee injected with cortisone by an orthopaedic specialist in NZ. The damage included having an anterior cruciate torn off the bone. It had been brought about originally by the plane crash in 1983 (narrated in Part Two).

Gordie Brown sold all my equipment on my behalf by auction during the forthcoming weeklong period of race training. All my Head skis, my Head boots, my curved racing poles, my helmet, my racing suit.

For the record, my best results in international Masters events were these:

SLALOM

Canadian Nationals 2000	GOLD
Canadian Nationals 1999	GOLD
Canadian Nationals 1997	GOLD
World Masters Alpine Open 1996	GOLD
FIS International Masters Cup 1996	SILVER

US Nationals 1995	BRONZE
FIS International Masters Cup 1994	SILVER
US Nationals 1994	SILVER
FIS International Masters Cup 1993	SILVER
FIS International Master Cup 1993	BRONZE
Canadian Nationals 1992	SILVER
Canadian Nationals 1991	GOLD

TOTAL: **5 GOLD, 5 SILVER, 2 BRONZE**

GIANT SLALOM

FIS Criterium Mondial 2002 (Abetone, Italy)	**BRONZE**
FIS International Seniors Cup 2002	SILVER
FIS International Masters Cup 2002	SILVER
FIS International Masters Cup 2001	BRONZE
Canadian Nationals 2000	GOLD
Canadian Nationals 1999	GOLD
FIS International Masters Cup 1997	SILVER
US Nationals 1997	SILVER
Canadian Open Nationals 1997	GOLD
World Masters Alpine Open 1996	GOLD
FIS International Masters Cup 1996	GOLD
US Nationals 1995	BRONZE
Canadian Nationals 1994	SILVER
Canadian Nationals 1992	BRONZE

TOTAL: **5 GOLD, 5 SILVER, 4 BRONZE**

Super G

Canadian Nationals 2004	GOLD
US National Speed series 2004 SG #1	GOLD
US National Speed Series 2004 SG #2	GOLD
FIS Criterium Mondial 2002 (Abetone, Italy)	**GOLD**
Canadian Nationals 2003	GOLD
Canadian Nationals 2002	GOLD
FIS Criterium Mondial 2001 (Park City, Utah)	**GOLD**
Canadian Nationals 2000	GOLD
FIS Criterium Mondial 1997 (Copper Mountain, CO)	**GOLD**
US Nationals 1997	GOLD
Canadian Open Nationals 1997	GOLD
World Masters Alpine Open 1996	GOLD
Canadian Nationals 1994	GOLD
Canadian Nationals 1992	SILVER
FIS Criterium Mondial 1991 (Winter Park, CO)	**SILVER**

TOTAL: **13** GOLD, **2** SILVER

Downhill

(Restricted to Canada and USA; Not Recognized by FIS Masters)

Canadian Nationals 2005	SILVER
Canadian Nationals 2004	GOLD
US National Speed Series 2004 DH #1	GOLD
US National Speed Series 2004 DH #2	GOLD
Canadian Nationals 2003	GOLD

Canadian Nationals 2002	GOLD
Canadian Nationals 2001	GOLD
Canadian Nationals 2000	GOLD
US Nationals 1998	GOLD
US Nationals 1995	GOLD
US Nationals 1992	SILVER

TOTAL: **9 GOLD, 2 SILVER**

GRAND TOTAL: **32 GOLD, 14 SILVER, 6 BRONZE**

8. ACKNOWLEDGEMENTS TO SUPPLIERS

During the period of my Masters Ski Racing I was, at different times, sponsored by:

Salomon Canada (skis and boots) courtesy of Jacques Morel and the chief distributor in Montreal, someone called Mingo (to both of whom I had to explain my defection);

Head Canada (skis and boots) courtesy of Robin McLeish (one-time member of the Canadian Ski Team);

Head New Zealand (skis, jackets, racing suit) courtesy of Adrian Farnsworth one-time member of the NZ Ski Team);

Dominator wax (racing wax);

Carerra goggles.

Silver medal at Winter Park, 1991

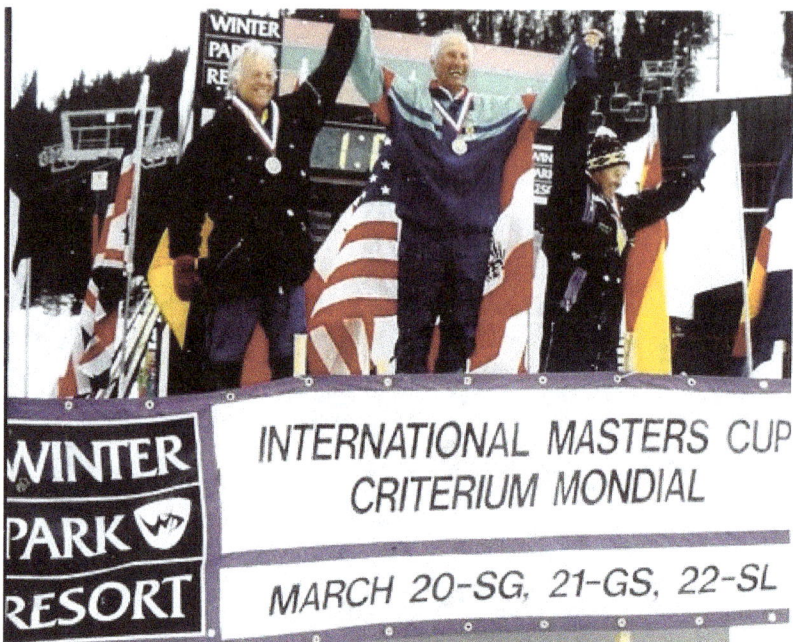

INTERNATIONAL MASTERS CUP
CRITERIUM MONDIAL

MARCH 20-SG, 21-GS, 22-SL

Above: On the podium at Winter Park, 1991

Below: Park City Super G, 2001

Above: Park City Super G, 2001

Below: Abetone Super G, 2002

Abetone Podium Gold, 2002

Above: Abetone Podium Giant Slalom, 2002

Below: Racing Downhill in 2005 Canadian Nationals aged 74

THREAD 4: WOMEN IN MY LIFE

1. BACKGROUND

Of my many relationships with women – sexual relationships, that is – most were of brief duration: giving way to mutual attraction by going to bed with one another. Just a few were of longer duration: a month or two; or even a couple of years. Or, in a couple of cases, lasting for more than that.

My story is about two of the latter: Ingrid and Juliet.

First let me fill in a bit of background.

At the beginning of 1954, I had married my childhood sweetheart, Molly (as she was then called). We had been boyfriend and girlfriend from the age of about twelve, with a few brief breaks when we were both at Auckland Teachers College. At the time we were married, in 1954, we were both virgins, having repressed the desire for sex by a little animated fondling when opportunity arose.

Then, probably on our honeymoon, Molly became pregnant, first with one child, then with another. And you know what that does for sexual relations. It wasn't until four years later, while we were living in Sydney, that Molly grew desperately ill with asthma and I had to move her and the boys back to Canberra, while I commuted weekly from Sydney.

At that point Molly suggested I take a lover, or two, to satisfy

116

my sexual needs. Generous? Yes. But I declined. For two main reasons: first, I might injure her feelings; second, I didn't know how, having been sexually inexperienced prior to marriage.

However, that set us thinking and talking about the merits of a so-called "open marriage".

It wasn't until several years later, when our sons were about to enter their teenage years, that we put it into practice: covertly at first, then more openly.

And then Molly confessed her lesbian tendencies. I'd suspected that for years; but eventually Molly was quite open about it. That led to our decision to go our own ways, though I supported her financially for twenty-seven years.

And that leads me to my first little story.

2. THE STORY OF INGRID

I first met Ingrid when she answered an ad I'd placed in the local newspaper, *The Whistler Question*, giving details of rental space available in our newly built house at Whistler. She was a gorgeous young woman: a qualified ski instructor from Ontario. She had also earned a degree in agriculture with an emphasis on environmental science.

It didn't take us long to become close friends. We skied together a lot: first at Whistler, and Blackcomb, then at resorts in the BC interior such as Apex Mountain just north of the border with the US. She introduced me to her brothers both of whom lived in British Columbia, and I introduced her to my sons. I met her parents and older sisters when we went to visit them in London, Ontario. By this time, I had fallen in love with Ingrid. And we became lovers.

We spent some time in Theodosia where on one occasion Ingrid helped me sort some naturally seeded oysters, the result of an unusually hot summer.

The time came when we decided to move in together: first into an apartment above the Upper Levels Highway in West Vancouver, then into a townhouse in North Vancouver. About a year or so in each, as I remember it. Ingrid was appointed to a fairly senior position in one of British Columbia's largest environmental firms. And I, of course, continued to teach at Simon Fraser University.

Then came my sabbatical leave in 1984. We decided that it was time to introduce Ingrid to my family "Down Under": Australia and New Zealand.

We flew via Hawaii, Tahiti, Rarotonga and Aitutaki, to Sydney, then on to Adelaide where we were met by my youngest brother, Murray. He took us up to the farm where he and his wife, Heather, were living. At that time, Murray was teaching by day at a college north of Adelaide while Heather was a librarian at a local school. I well remember us, Ingrid and me, being taken on a walk round the farm by their precocious young son, Guy (now named Connor) and being regaled about the hazards of trying to raise geese in an environment replete with foxes. Guy was about two or three at the time and a great little conversationalist.

We visited Merle and Neil Thornton in Melbourne; and while there met their actress daughter, Sigrid, (my one-time ward with her brother Harold) and her future husband, Tom Burstall.

We travelled up to Sydney where we stayed with Jim Farrell and his first wife, Jan, and their two boys. We visited the sights, from the Opera House out to the south heads of Sydney Harbor.

From there we hired a campervan and drove northward up the coast towards Brisbane diverting, on several occasions, from the main highway down a little sandy track to get to a coastal beach for the night. I remember Ingrid's dismay, as we neared Brisbane, at finding that pineapples didn't grow on trees but on low leafy, spikey, plants up to 5 feet tall.

We stayed briefly with Brian Wilson and his wife, my one-time partner at Theodosia and ex-Vice President at Simon Fraser, by then Vice-Chancellor at the University of Brisbane.

We returned to Sydney just in time to catch the plane to New Zealand.

Then began our tour of my home country. It all began in the Auckland area where we visited or stayed with the rest of my family: my mother; and my other younger brother, Neville, and his wife Beryl, at their house in Manly, north of Auckland, where Neville was the local pharmacist. As I remember it, my youngest brother, Murray, came over from Australia with his wife Heather. At least, they feature in a photo, together with Neville's daughters, and Ingrid, in Neville's spa pool. We visited Piha on the west coast, and went sailing with brother Neville and friend Wilton Willis.

We took our time and covered the country pretty thoroughly, from Matauri Bay (just north of the farm that is now occupied by the famed golf course, Kauri Cliffs) and the Cavalli Islands in the north, to Queenstown in the South Island via Hot Water Beach, Coromandel, Rotorua and the nearby thermal areas such as Waimangu and Wairakei.

In the Coromandel area, we stayed some time in Neville and

Beryl's beach house in Pauanui and went on day-hikes with my friend Doug Johansen.

Ingrid was very impressed by the magic of the thermal areas around Lake Rotorua, and the volcanic mountains Ngaruahoe, Tongariro and Ruapehu.

The South Island offered its own magic. We met various of my old skiing friends, dating back to the sixties, and stayed with several of them. Most of this took place in 1984 and early 1985.

We returned to Vancouver in time for me to teach again at Simon Fraser.

Sometime in 1985, we were visited by Neville and Beryl. They helped us move into a rental house near Pinecrest Estates, some miles south of Whistler, with easy access to the mountains as well as Vancouver.

It was in the winter season at the end of 1985 that Ingrid took up a post as ski instructor at Whistler Mountain.

3. INGRID'S LIFE-THREATENING ACCIDENT

In March 1986, while staying at Pinecrest and working on the manuscript of a book, I received an urgent phone call from my doctor at the medical clinic in Whistler. It was about Ingrid.

She had been leading a group of children down a beginner's run when she was hit by an out-of-control skier named Chris Wilcox at about waist height. Not only was he out of control; he was skiing extremely fast. He had been participating in speed trials higher on the mountain before being dismissed by the coaches as a peril to himself and others. Angry at his dismissal, he chose the quickest

120

and easiest way down the mountain, ignoring signs advising that this was a beginner's run and cautioning against fast skiing. He skied so fast that he was taking air off blind bumps, and eventually crashed into Ingrid.

All this and other facts of the case emerged in the Supreme Court of British Columbia when the case known as "Wypkema versus Wilcox" was heard some months later. Wilcox had been charged by the police with reckless skiing.

Meantime, back to the call I received from my doctor. He told me that Ingrid had suffered terrible injuries, that they were trying to stabilize her before putting her in an ambulance to take her down to the hospital in North Vancouver, and said that he had asked the drivers to pick me up on the main highway just outside Pinecrest Estates.

I acted accordingly, running out to the highway, then waited to hear the sound of the ambulance siren wailing its way down the valley. The ambulance stopped and bundled me in at the back so I could keep an eye on Ingrid. Miles later, we were passing some little lakes just before the road descends to the nearest town of Squamish when I knocked on the door separating me from the driver's compartment and told them that Ingrid needed urgent attention. She was fading fast. They gave her an injection to resuscitate her. Then they resumed their rush down the highway.

We were only about half way down to the North Shore Hospital when they swung off into the little hospital at Squamish and rushed Ingrid to the emergency department where we were met by a doctor. He took one look at Ingrid, decided she was drowning in her own blood, and without hesitating further, lifted up her arm and, using a scalpel to cut an incision in her chest, inserted a tube into her chest cavity and began to drain the rapidly accumulating blood. I watched in dismay.

They kept her overnight. Then next morning the ambulance resumed its journey down to the North Shore Hospital. There she underwent a more thorough examination.

She had suffered a shattered forearm that needed to be put together with dozens of staples, a broken collarbone, several broken ribs, and a punctured lung. She was in the North Shore Hospital for some quite some time before being deemed fit for release.

Meantime, I had gone back to Pinecrest. I went to see the RCMP at Whistler who were eager to prosecute Wilcox. Wilcox had been heard in a local pub, on the evening of the accident, boasting about his exploits and referring to the "silly bitch" who had got in his way.

I also contacted the Head of the Whistler Ski Patrol, Roger McCarthy, (a fellow-New Zealander friend of mine), and with the local police sergeant's co-operation, tried to reconstruct the parameters of the accident. How fast must Wilcox have been skiing to hit Ingrid at that height (a cut in her ski pants at the thigh level gave evidence of that)? A couple of ski patrollers tried to duplicate his speed. But they couldn't ski fast enough to catch air on the bump. Then I put on my 225 cm Head Downhill skis and took a run. I managed to imitate Wilcox's airtime and was timed by an RCMP officer, using a speed gun, at just on 75 kph.

That was enough evidence to supply to the Court as an explanation of the horrific injuries Ingrid had sustained. The RCMP brought criminal charges against Wilcox.

The Court hearing lasted a full week. I attended every day, listening attentively to the evidence and advising the prosecutor (Sandy Ross by name) when necessary about lines he might pursue. At one point, I noticed the presence of two well-dressed young gentlemen who were listening very closely and taking copious notes. I asked Sandy if he could find out their identities. They turned out to be representatives of the Wilcox family's insurance company. What were they doing, and why were they doing it? These were questions I was to pursue at a later point when issues of financial responsibility arose.

Before then, however, Judge John van der Hoop had delivered his verdict. Wilcox was found guilty of reckless skiing and showing "a wanton and willful disregard for the safety of others." He sentenced Wilcox to seven days in jail, two years' probation, two hundred hours of community work, and no skiing for a year. It was a precedent-setting verdict for Canada.

No mention, however, of financial compensation for the treatment Ingrid had received in hospital; or for the injury and pain Ingrid herself had suffered. It was, after all, a criminal court, not a civil one.

This did not satisfy my sense of justice. Accordingly, I approached the ICBC (Insurance Company of British Columbia).

Eventually, I was referred to their legal department. Their ruling, initially, was that they had no authority to intervene in the case. I asked to see their founding legislation and was supplied with the appropriate documents. I read them carefully and came to the conclusion that members of the ICBC were misreading a couple of the clauses therein. I went back to the legal department and put my case to the most senior man in charge. Eventually, he agreed with me.

Consequence? The Wilcox family's insurance company was made to pay about $80,000 to be split between the hospital and Ingrid (with Ingrid getting rather less than the lion's share).

All the events recounted so far, having to do with to do with Ingrid's accident and its aftermath in the Supreme Court, or relating to my dealings with the ICBC, occurred just after Ingrid and I had parted and gone our own ways.

The reasons leading to this may have been multiple. But for the most part they had to do with the age gap between us, Ingrid's desire for children of her own, and my reluctance to start a new family. At any event, sometime in 1985 we decided to separate. I was emotionally shattered at the time.

But we eventually became friends again and have remained so ever since. After a long period retailing works of art in Vancouver, she has now returned to Ontario where she has recently accepted an appointment as Garden Coordinator in The Bruce Botanical Food Gardens.

4. THE STORY OF JULIET

I first met the Fisher girls – the oldest, Rosemary, the twins Juliet and Merilyn, and the youngest, Deryn – in 1954. Their mother, Barbara, had been a fellow student of Philosophy the year before. She had taken classes, along with me and Rom Harre, in 1953.

A spellbindingly beautiful woman in her early thirties, Barbara had returned to the university to take a combined degree in English and Philosophy. I found it hard to take my eyes off her. Or was it the broad-brimmed hats she wore? Or the combination of those hats with her stunning eyes? At all events, towards the end of the year we became friends.

As explained in Part One, section 4, I graduated with a first-class honours degree at the end of 1953 and got married to Molly soon after, in March 1954. Then, sometime later that year came the visit to Auckland University of Professor Gilbert Ryle and, as became an academic of his distinction, Gilbert gave a couple of widely attended lectures. At the end of one of these he introduced me to his old friend from Oxford, the Vice-Chancellor Kenneth Maidment, telling him that I had just been awarded a PhD scholarship to the Australian National University in Canberra.

Barbara was listening with interest. She knew that I was married and that Molly was already pregnant with our first son, Gresham. She approached me before the evening was over, and suggested that I might find living on a scholarship a bit of a financial strain, and hence might like to accept her offer of free accommodation in the basement flat of her rather grand residence on Orakei Road in Remuera, a flash suburb of Auckland.

As already explained, I accepted gratefully, offering in return to help Barbara with the gardening.

It was then that I met her four daughters. They, of course, were entranced by meeting my baby son, Gresham, who had been born in October after a difficult birth, at Greenlane Hospital.

At that time, I was still teaching in New Lynn and making my way to and fro on a new Japanese Sun motorbike. On occasions,

Juliet met me at the garden gate and accompanied me up to the little basement apartment Molly and I were sharing. She would take a break from playing with her sisters. Maybe it was to find an excuse to see the new baby.

After about five months, Molly and I and Gresham took off for Canberra. I kept in touch with Barbara on occasions: about her graduation and subsequent appointment to the Auckland Teacher's College, and very occasionally about the careers being pursued by her daughters.

It came as no great surprise when, sometime in early 1960 I think it was, I heard from Barbara expressing some concern about Juliet. Juliet, she told me, had graduated from Epsom Girls Grammar and had travelled to Sydney intent on studying Contemporary Dance with Margaret Barr. Margaret was one of the more distinguished students of the critically acclaimed founder of that style of dance, Martha Graham, (noted performers of whose works included Mikhail Baryshnikov, Margot Fonteyn, and Rudolf Nureyev).

Juliet, Barbara told me, was lonely. She was staying in the Sydney YWCA and had no real friends. Could I please invite Juliet down to Canberra for a weekend or so?

At the time, I was still teaching for three days per week at the University of New South Wales in Sydney and driving down to Canberra, most weeks, to be with the family. These were the days when Molly and my two boys had gone to Canberra so as to afford relief from the pollution in Miranda and had taken refuge in a house on Fouveaux Street, part way up Mt Ainslie.

I was happy to oblige. I picked up Juliet late on the Thursday night and drove her down to Canberra. We talked at length. I expressed surprise that someone as intellectually gifted as Juliet would choose dance as a profession. By the time we stopped for a break at Lake George, just south of Goulburn, I thought I understood. We stood, watching the moonlight rise over the lake where its beauty seemed to me to reflect that of Juliet herself. Then we proceeded to Canberra.

Over the forthcoming weekend, Juliet and I took several walks on the mountain just opposite. Without any trace of self-consciousness, Juliet slipped her hand into mine. Repeatedly.

By the end of the weekend, Molly was aware of the growing affection between us and remarked on the fact. "You are in love with her," she said. I did not deny it.

But our futures were already seemingly sealed: Juliet's in contemporary dance (she was bound, late in 1960, for New York to study with Martha Graham); mine in Philosophy (I was destined to go to Oxford in a few months' time, just missing Juliet when Molly and I and the boys arrived in London at the beginning of 1961 to stay with Barbara and her husband George for a few days). Nothing had been said between us. But I never forgot Juliet's lingering look when I left her at the railway station in Canberra for her return to Sydney.

5. A Brief Love Affair With Juliet

It was some eight years before I met Juliet again. By then, Molly and I were more than halfway home on our circumnavigation of the globe. My eight-month sabbatical from Auckland had taken us to

Canada for about two months, the US for about five, and the UK for about a month. It was early 1968.

While I was visiting the University of Minnesota, Molly had had her little affair with my poet-philosopher friend Keith Gunderson. Now it was time for her to reciprocate. We had already been to Norway where we spent some time in Oslo and one of the west-coast fjords.

Sweden was next on the list. We had arranged through Barbara to spend some time with Juliet in Stockholm. Mindful of the affection that Molly had seen develop between Juliet and me back in 1960, Molly made the decision to fly on to Helsinki for a few days ahead of me, leaving me alone with Juliet.

Juliet had already had a distinguished performing career as a soloist with the Martha Graham Company in New York and had moved on to become a founding member and soloist with the Cullbergbaletten in Stockholm.

Things developed rapidly between the two of us. By the second day, we could hardly keep our hands off each other. When the time came for me to fly on and rejoin Molly on our way back to New Zealand, it was with considerable reluctance that I left Juliet. But once again, our careers drove us apart.

6. INTERLUDE: AN EVENTFUL TRIP BACK TO AUCKLAND

I rejoined Molly in Helsinki, stayed a day or two, then flew off to the Soviet Union where our first touch-down was at the rebuilt city of Petrograd. By this time, Molly had to be hospitalized for several days leaving me to explore the city by myself. I accepted an invitation from a couple of American academics and their wives to visit the magnificent Hermitage Museum, but soon excused myself from their company. The men, in particular, were arrogant, ignorant, and insensitive fools, making derogatory remarks about Russian history, in front of our Russian taxi-driver. I found them embarrassing. I had met their likes before; and I was to meet their likes many times afterward when I eventually took up residence in Canada.

I lingered at the museum, taking hours to study its contents from the Egyptian antiquities, to Catherine the Greats' collection, sculptures by Rodin, and many Picassos. I explored the magnificent underground and took trips out to several of its suburbs. All while waiting for Molly to be released. Somewhere or other she had contracted a kidney disease of such seriousness that our neighbor at home in Remuera, Dr McLaurin (the first to perform kidney operations in New Zealand) extolled the Soviet health system saying that they must have worked wonders to have kept her alive.

Molly and I had intended to visit Moscow, but time did not allow.

We flew on, instead, to the city of Yerevan, in Armenia. There we were met by a philosopher, head of the Philosophy Department in Yerevan and a member of a group of Soviet Academicians who had visited Auckland some time before. We'd become friends, as philosophers, back then. Nevertheless, we were surprised when he met us at the airport with a grand bouquet of flowers for Molly and a bottle of Armenian brandy for me. We were whisked off to the upper private dining room of the hotel Yerevan where we met one of his ex-students, now working as a guide for Russian Tourism. A magnificent dinner was to follow.

The guide, whose name I now forget, invited us to dine with his parents the next night. It was an uproarious occasion. The food was great, and the number of toasts with Armenian brandy too many to count. "To all men of good will," was his father's repeated chant. And I had to reciprocate with raised glass. I had to give up before feeling too tipsy.

Next day, as I remember it, our guide took us to meet some fellow students of his in an outlying village where I was dismayed at the quality of the construction: the stairways were already crumbling and rickety. But the students to whom we were introduced greeted us warmly. Similarly at the next village we visited. And the next.

At the end of our stay in Yerevan we flew to the oil city of Baku on the Caspian Sea, then on to Tashkent, Samarkand, and Bukhara, all three in southern Soviet Republic of Uzbekistan, and all three on the Great Silk Road from China to Europe. Each is a magical city with magnificent buildings and engaging people.

But this is not the place to elaborate on any of them.

Better to tell briefly about our ongoing flight from Tashkent to Kabul in Afghanistan. We were about to descend into the city's airport when the plane in which we were flying suddenly assumed an extremely steep angle. We were at about 10,000 ft of altitude, and could see a virtual layer of huge buzzards circling below us. We were seated on the left side of the aircraft, when we saw one of them wheeling around into the flight path of the plane. It was about to collide with the cockpit of the airplane, which would have killed both pilots and all the passengers, when the pilot at the controls diverted our path so that the buzzard hit the left-hand front spoiler with a loud crash.

Molly and I clung to each other thinking that was the end. Our only thought was of our children back home, staying with friends in Auckland. The plane continued on its near-vertical path towards the ground, then pulled out and just made it on to the runway. All of us were stunned. It took some minutes before disembarkation began. Even the pilot and co-pilot preceded us. By the time we clambered out the two pilots were inspecting the damage. We approached them and were offered an explanation by the American co-pilot. We owed our lives, he said, to the quick reflexes of the Afghan pilot. I pulled on one of the feathers. It was effectively "glued" to the shattered metal as a consequence of the heat generated by the impact.

It took us two or three nights in our hotel to recover from the trauma. On a few occasions, however, we ventured outside and took in the sights. And the people around us. The women in particular were stunningly beautiful, dressed in Western-style clothes, and the men impressively handsome with short beards. The whole country was under the influence of the Soviet regime, and largely financed by them. The prime minister, at the time, was a man named Taraki who, as a Communist, made efforts to improve secular education and redistribute land. Little wonder, we thought, that the capital looked so peaceful.

The US, it is true, was starting to undermine the pro-Soviet regime by pouring money and weapons to the mujahideen rebels, and forcing the Soviets to eventually abandon Afghanistan. But their final retreat came many years later, in 1987.

From Kabul we flew to New Delhi where we were faced by the

same sort of poverty and destitution that we had last seen in 1960 when our vessel called in at Columbo, Sri Lanka. Beggars were lying in the streets, stretching their hands out for money. And that was under the relatively liberal Indian Prime Minister, Indira Ghandi. What a stark contrast with Kabul, we thought!

Next it was on to Bangkok, the predominately Buddhist capital of Thailand. We stayed there a few days. Then it was off to Phnom Penh in Cambodia. A beautiful country it seemed to us at the time: well-dressed peasants riding bicycles through peaceful farmland on the way from the airport to the capital. Prince Norodom Sihanouk was effectively in power at the time. We visited his palace and took photos of his two elephants standing on guard. We had hoped to fly up to the largest religious monument in the world, Angor Wat, but had missed the weekly flight by a day. We contented ourselves by purchasing some of the temple rubbings, etched in charcoal on rice paper.

Cambodia was about to join Vietnam in US-induced carnage. But Nixon was already denying any involvement. Before we left Phnom Phen, however, we had proof to the contrary. Our guide took us down to the western bank of the Mekong River, and there displayed the wreckages of several US planes that the Cambodians claimed to have shot down. It was a year or so before the US acknowledged that it had begun a four-year devastating secret carpet-bombing of the countryside. It caused the socio-political upheaval that eventually led to the installation of the disastrous Pol Pot regime.

We were to witness further confirmation of the US barbarism being wreaked on South-East Asia when we flew over Vietnam en route to our next stop in Hong Kong. I don't know at what altitude we were flying; but it was high enough for us to witness huge flotillas of American planes raining their bombs on the already devastated country below. Vast clouds of smoke and fire followed their progress. My antipathy for American foreign policy grew by the day.

From Hong Kong south through Darwin, Sydney, and eventually home to Auckland our journey was uneventful. But the bitter taste for Western foreign policy at the time remained. New Zealand's military force in Vietnam was at its peak in 1968, having been enhanced by sending a battery of artillery (against my and other's protests) in 1966.

My stance on matters to do with US foreign policy, in particular, continued to harden when we went to Canada at the end of 1969. In 1972 Nixon launched what came to be known as "The Christmas Bombing": the bombing of north Vietnam's capital Hanoi. At that time Pierre Trudeau – the father of the current prime minister of Canada, Justin – was himself prime minister of our newly adopted country. Knowing of his liberal sympathies, I decided to approach Pierre with a view to asking him to intervene personally with Nixon requesting him to desist his latest hegemonic aggression. I gathered a small group of like-minded people together and between us wrote Pierre a large Christmas card, about 6 foot by 8 foot, conveying what we wanted him to say. We had reason to believe that he was staying in West Vancouver with his wife, Margaret Sinclair's, parents, so stood outside their residence for some hours hoping he would turn up. Then a neighbor told us Trudeau and his in-laws had already gone up to Whistler. Since I was the only member of our group planning to drive up there that night, I volunteered to take the card with me. It was two days before

Christmas. So the next day, having heard that Pierre had gone up the gondola to ski, I waited at the bottom of the gondola for him to return. The last gondola of the day ground to a halt. No Trudeau. That's when I was told that he had caught a helicopter down to the parking lot close to the Sinclair's cabin. Hence off to the parking lot. There I was confronted by an RCMP officer. What was my mission, he asked? "You can't talk to the PM on Christmas Eve," he replied. "I think it is up to the PM, not you, to decide whether or not he wants to speak to me," I responded. Off he went along the board-walk. A few minutes later, he returned. "The PM will be with you shortly." Pierre turned up about ten minutes later. Heavy snow was plummeting out the dark sky. I introduced myself and we talked international politics for about forty minutes. He reported having already protested to Nixon twice, but said he'd be prepared to do so again. I was immensely impressed by his intelligence and demeanor. And integrity.

A few weeks later, it was all over. To what extent, if any, Trudeau's intervention, or mine for that matter, made a difference, I know not.

7. LIVING TOGETHER AT LAST

Back to the story of Juliet. When I had my little affair in Stockholm with Juliet, I had no expectation of ever being with her again. True, I had seen her for morning coffee very soon after she had given birth to her first child, Ben. But that was that.

Meantime I had had that affair of several years with Ingrid, and had eventually entered into my second marriage in 1996, the one with Belinda (see Part 2). But that marriage broke up in mid-2000. And as a result I had decided to return to New Zealand.

More than a third of a century had passed before Juliet and I were able to be together again.

The year was 2001. It was early January and I had flown down to Auckland for a week in order to line up builders for my new house at Omaha Beach. I phoned Juliet's youngest sister, Deryn Holt, to tell her and her husband, Alf, that I was in town. They invited me to dine with them on the Saturday night, the evening before I was due to fly back to Vancouver.

In the course of conversation, I asked about Juliet. "Didn't you know? She's back in Auckland," was Deryn's reply. "I'd love to see her again," I responded. "That's easily arranged," Deryn responded. "I'll invite her for dinner, too."

Deryn went on to explain that Juliet had recently divorced her second husband and had made the decision to bring their mother, Barbara, back from Oxford to Auckland, and once back had decided to stay herself. All this, of course, was news to me.

Saturday evening came. And I met Juliet again. She was as enchanting as ever. Before the evening was over, we had taken our leave and gone back to where I was staying. That was it. We resumed our relationship as if it never ceased since our days together in Stockholm.

The next morning, I flew back to Vancouver.

Over the next three or four weeks, Juliet and I were constantly in touch by phone. The long-distance charges were mounting: several hundred dollars each. Eventually, I said: "Look, darling. If our relationship is going to go anywhere, I think we should try a trial

135

'honeymoon'. How about meeting for week or so in Hawaii?" Juliet readily agreed. We met in Honolulu, then flew to the Big Island for a week. What a wonderful time!

Just one thing slightly worried me during our otherwise idyllic time together: she smoked. For how long had she been hooked? I didn't remember her being that way when she was in Stockholm. But she suggested it was virtually pandemic among the professional dance community, particularly at the London School of Contemporary Dance. I said I couldn't live with that and warned her of the serious health consequences of her continuing.

She said she'd give it up before we met again in Auckland. And subsequently she sent me photos of her lighting a little offering of her "last packet of sigs" as she sent it floating out with the tide from a small cove near Herne Bay. I believed her at the time, though later it all turned out to be a bit of a charade

By the time we parted from Hawaii, I had decided to cut down on the remainder of my ski-racing schedule. I came back to Auckland on the 21/22 March 2001, straight into the waiting arms of my love, Juliet. It seemed at that time that she'd kept her promise about stopping smoking.

Juliet met me at the airport with a little card that I've kept until this day. It read:

> *Ray,*
> *Welcome ashore my darling,*
> *Into our future of adventures together,*
> *And into embraces of eternal ecstasy,*
> *And timeless tenderness.*
> *Juliet. XXXXXX*

On my arriving in Auckland, we moved into her little apartment in Herne Bay and stayed there until my house at Omaha Beach was ready for occupation in late October 2001.

Meantime, Juliet had accepted a position as teacher of Contemporary Dance Technique at Unitec, in Mt Albert, where she taught until 2003. She also became a teacher of Pilates Technique in Parnell, more or less for the same period, 2001-2003. In 2004 she taught Contemporary Dance Technique at the University of Auckland where she became a long-standing friend and dance-partner with Timothy Gordon. All this time, Juliet kept her apartment in Herne Bay and spent her long weekends with me at Omaha.

But much of this time, Juliet was being exposed to the old temptation of smoking, which was as prevalent among dancers in NZ as in the rest of the world. She also found it especially easy to succumb when she stayed overnight, on occasions, with her twin sister, Merilyn, who also smoked.

How did this resumption affect our relationship? It proved to be something of a problem from time to time, especially when she returned from Auckland to stay with me for a long weekend. But it started to fade once she sold her apartment in Herne Bay and began to live with me full-time.

Besides, now that she was relieved of her teaching duties, we started to travel more frequently. We had both acquired Subaru 4-wheel drives: I a station wagon suitable for driving in snow country such as Ruapehu and the ski slopes in the South Island; she a Blitzen sedan, more low-slung and suitable for driving in the city. We would swap when circumstances dictated.

We drove up to the North Cape via the West Coast via the Kauri forest and the 90-mile beach, then back down the East Coast via Keri Keri and Whangarei with numerous stops in both directions.

Another time we drove south. First it was off to Rotorua, Tauranga, and the East Cape to Wellington, then via the ferry to Picton and the Kaikoura Peninsular where we took a brilliant helicopter trip for whale watching. The helicopter proved to be a good choice compared with that of a boat. No crowds, no tossing by the waves; seeing multiple whales breaching from their deep dives. That's what we saw from the helicopter. Besides the views of the snow-capped ranges were absolutely magnificent.

Then it was on to Christchurch and to the South Island ski fields: Mt Hutt, Cardrona, Treble Cone, and Coronet. It was in resorts like these that Juliet gradually learned to ski, somewhat trepidatiously at first, then with increasing confidence. Treblecone, near Lake Wanaka, came last on the list as we began our drive up the West coast of the South Island, then across the channel to Wellington and up the coast via New Plymouth and ultimately to Auckland. It was a wonderful way to virtually complete our circumnavigation of the country.

The next time we skied together we were visiting Whistler. It came about this way. We had joined an organization that arranged Home Exchanges for New Zealanders. It had members in most parts of the world who undertook to swap their homes with members in New Zealand. And one of these owned a house in Whistler that they were prepared to exchange, with ours in Omaha. "For free", as they say, for any period we chose to arrange. The Whistler exchange lasted just over a month. Plenty of time for Juliet to develop her skiing; to the point where she could ski with confidence down most "Green" runs, while I joined with old friends rocketing down "Black" runs. The facilities on Whistler Mountain, like those at nearby Blackcomb, were world-class as became those of a resort to be selected later as the venue for the 2010 Olympics. When the weather closed in, we took time to introduce Juliet to many of my old friends, Alfred Zielberger, Bobby Switzer, Randal Carpenter, Bud White, etc.

We repeated the home exchanges with other members several times again. At Silver Star on at least three occasions so that I could race in the Over The Hill Downhill (by then designated as the Canadian National Championships).

And with a couple from near Avignon, in the south of France. As always, exchanges included vehicles. So we were able to make extensive tours around the southern coast of France, taking in many of the relics from the Roman era.

It would take too long to tell much about our other overseas trips. But these included: London, Brighton, Kenya, Tanzania, Turkey, Croatia, Langkawi (northern Malaysia), several times to Queensland (to Cooktown, and twice to Cairns), and finally, in 2009, British Columbia and Alberta.

Those to London and Brighton were principally to visit Juliet's children, Elena and Ben and their families/friends

Visits to Kenya and Tanzania were principally to see the wildlife, starting with a flight from Dubai to Nairobi and exiting via a week or so in the Island of Zanzibar. Not only did we see the so-called "Big Five" (the lions, leopards, rhinoceros, elephant, and Cape buffalo): we also saw many of them in action, feeding on lesser beasts that

139

abounded in the two countries.

For example, on our very first evening, we saw a pride of lions stalking a herd of zebras; and on the very next morning watched their baby cubs playing with zebra heads and carcasses. And two weeks later, in Tanzania's Ngorongoro Valley (about 19 km across) we saw a pride of lions and cubs hemming in a similar motorized van and preventing them from moving because of the proximity of their cubs and lionesses. Numerous other species of predators and prey abounded: including hyenas, crocodiles, foxes, wild boars, and giraffes, in both countries, plus eagles, vultures and other magnificent birds.

The "native" peoples, principally the Matai, who lived mainly in the countryside, seemed to be living a timeless existence in a timeless landscape.

Turkey and Croatia were entirely different in character. Both gave evidence of a much more recent past. In Turkey, the museums or ruins of ancient cities such as Istanbul, Ephesus and Ankara bore witness to Roman origins, while the hot-air balloons of Cappadocia provided a wonderful opportunity to survey an ancient landscape.

In Croatia, the cities of Split and the walled city of Dubrovnik bore witness to much later origins. They came as a relatively welcome relief after a week of visiting the offshore islands up the coast in a well-crafted boat in which we experienced temperatures of over 38 degrees Celsius.

But the most memorable event in my mind was of a guided trip down one of the numerous intervening rivers flowing from the nearby mountains to the sea. Our craft was an inflatable dinghy. Our guide carried us down the river until we came to rapids that were too dangerous for us to navigate. Then we had to walk down to calmer water. There we encountered a deep pool. I chose to dive in from a rock about 15 feet high, to great applause from the watching spectators. The guide described me as the only man aged over 65 to do so.

Our three visits to Queensland were very different again. On one occasion we took a four-wheel drive up to Cooktown from Cairns and then back down the coast again via Aboriginal settlements that bore little evidence of twentieth century white occupation. Making it across crocodile-infested rivers only added to our sense of daring. Unfortunately, our intent of visiting the Great Barrier Reef was frustrated by bad weather on the other two occasions. We did make up for this on one occasion by taking a magnificent cable-car trip up to the mountaintop tourist village of Kuranda where we spent some time shopping before descending on the Kuranda Scenic Railway.

8. BRITISH COLUMBIA AND ALBERTA: MY LAST OVERSEAS VISIT

In 2009 Juliet and I decided to visit Canada again. She had joined me several times before so that I could race in Silver Star's National Downhill Championship. But that was always in the winter. She hadn't seen the beauties of the colors of the West Coast in the fall. Neither had she seen the wonders of the Canadian Rockies and its abundant wildlife.

Happily, our friend Jim Farrell had made his four-wheel-drive vehicle available for the month-long trip. We started by driving north of Vancouver up to Whistler, stopping en route at Shannon Falls, cascading down series of cliffs from 355 meters above the highway, and Brandywine Falls where the water plummets straight down about 70 meters to the creek below.

Once at Whistler itself we took the Peak to Peak Gondola from Whistler to Blackcomb, until recently (2017) the longest free-span lift in the world and still the highest above the ground (436 meters). It finally opened in 2007 and is truly magnificent as a viewing point for the valley below. We stayed at a friend's chalet for two or three days so as to be able to enjoy the splendors of Whistler Village itself.

Resuming our journey north, we next stopped 32 km north of Whistler at Nairn Falls where the Green River plunges from one pothole to another before resuming its steady path northward towards Pemberton. Then we drove north-east through the Indian Reservation of Mt Currie where we had an interesting conversation with an aggressive native Indian, one that we resolved by telling him of our NZ origins and that similar conflicts arose down there. Off we went through the mountains to Lillooet, then through Cache Creek, to Kamloops and, for a few days, to the Jim Farrell's chalet at Sun Peaks.

That gave us time to reassess our situation. I had skied there many times so knew our location fairly well. One route I had never taken before took us over the logging roads east of Sun Peaks; so we took that, stopping at various minor lakes on the way down to a highway that eventually connected us with the route to Jasper.

Just before coming to Jasper, we drove through the Mt Robson Provincial Park. Mt Robson itself is spectacular. At 3954m, it is the highest peak in the Canadian Rockies and the source of British Columbia's greatest river. The Fraser River rises from its headwaters on Robson to flow 1370 km down to Vancouver in the west. Vast numbers of wildlife abound there: including moose, mountain goats, elk, caribou, grizzlies and black bears.

We stayed at the town of Jasper for two nights taking the intervening day to travel north. The Ice-fields Highway from Jasper, down the Rocky Mountain Trench to Banff is reputedly one of the most spectacular in the world, offering views of glaciers coming down close to the highway on both sides.

We spent a night or so in the city of Banff before driving north again to Lake Louise.

Thence back to Vancouver via Golden and Revelstoke, Sicamous, Vernon, Kelowna, Penticton, and Princeton, to Hope and down the Fraser Valley. I forget what we did (if anything) in each of those towns, but several were familiar from our time staying in Vernon while skiing in Silver Star, and each had its own charm. Besides, the Okanagan Lake is the site of countless orchards and a blaze of color in the fall. "Peachland" it is known as.

We wanted to get back to Vancouver in time to catch various ferries up the coast towards Powell River and across to Vancouver Island to get to down to Denman Island. Timing was of the essence. I forget just how we did it; but I wanted Juliet to see the terrain that I had travelled almost weekly in the summer months in order to get to my log cabin in Theodosia Inlet. Denman Island was now the home of my good friend Brenda Finch who used to live at Potage Cove, about 2.5 miles from my cabin in Theodosia. She had moved to Denman Island after the death of her husband Bill Finch.

We stayed with Brenda for three or four days, planning to go on from Denman Island to drive down to the ferry terminal at

Nanaimo so as to catch our booked flight on Air New Zealand on the following Sunday.

That didn't happen, for reasons I will now explain. One afternoon, just after lunch, Juliet, Brenda, and I decided to go for a walk through the adjacent Provincial Park. At the furthest point of our hike, we came across a magnificent sight: a bald eagle was perched on the top of a nearby fir tree that was rooted in the rocks about 100 feet below the cliff top on which we were standing. We watched it intently for a few minutes, then set off to return to Brenda's cabin.

All went well for the first twenty minutes or so. Then, part way through a conversation with the two women, I found myself feeling giddy and unable to talk. I sat down on a nearby log. Five or so minutes later I was able to resume. I had just had the first of a series of intermittent strokes.

My strokes continued to recur at intervals before we got back to Brenda's cabin. Then I went to bed and slept for three quarters of an hour or so. On waking up, I felt fully refreshed and so joined the conversation in the living room. But then my symptoms recurred again. And again. And again.

On the Friday morning we left Brenda's and drove down to Nanaimo in time for the ferry back to Horseshoe Bay and Vancouver. No stroke symptoms occurred. Until we were comfortably seated on the ferry. Then soon after, an old friend from Whistler days, seated in the row immediately in front of us, turned and said, "Ray Bradley! What are you doing here?" I was in the middle of responding when the symptoms hit again. That happened twice during the 1.45 hours trip back to the mainland. It was clear that I hadn't recovered.

144

On Sunday morning, I delayed responding to Juliet's urging to have myself checked in at the Vancouver General Hospital to see if I was fit to fly that evening, until after lunch. At about 3 pm, I checked in at the Emergency Department. They sent me for a CT scan. Twice. As the time for checking in for our flight approached, I grew increasingly nervous. Flight check-in time approached. And passed. Then came the verdict. "You're not going anywhere. We're preparing a hospital bed."

So it was that I spent a full week until being deemed fit to travel, only gradually recovering my ability to speak, eat, or walk. Poor Juliet had to deal with the complexities of negotiating with our insurance company and having our booking changed to the following Sunday. Meanwhile the medical diagnosis had been given. I had suffered what the doctors there called a major ischaemic "Stuttering Stroke".

I was wheeled from the hospital in a stretcher, carried by ambulance to the aircraft, and put in a comfortable bed alongside Juliet for the trip back to Auckland.

So much for my first stroke. It involved a blockage of the basal ganglia at the back of my brain.

Since then, at the time of writing (20 July 2018), I have been hospitalized in the North Shore Hospital on six occasions, on three of which my sons have been told by medical authorities that I had only a few days to live. But I continue to cheat death.

Even that was threatened by a so-called "near-drowning experience." That occurred a couple of summers ago when my son Gresham, plus Juliet's daughter, Elena, her daughter Stella, and her partner Lou, decided to go swimming in the nearby Whangateau

145

Harbor. I decided to accompany them, wading rather than swimming. The tide started going out, increasingly fast. The swiftness of the current left me pawing for a grip on the sand until I could no longer maintain contact.

My head dipped under the water and I started inhaling. "So this is what it's like to be a fish," was my first thought. "I'm drowning. And it's almost euphoric," was my second.

I had continued to struggle towards the shore where I was eventually noticed by Lou. I was on all-fours, but unable to raise my head above the water. By the time she, Elena, and Gresham rescued me I had both lungs pretty much filled with water. A watching neighbor called the ambulance. A motorized one turned up. The attendants were in the process of helping me evacuate my lungs of frothy pink water when the Westpac Helicopter landed and whisked me off to the North Shore Hospital for further treatment.

Needless to say, I recovered.

9. JULIET'S DEMISE

Sadly, however, my darling Juliet has died.

Many years after quitting smoking, she developed COPD (Chronic Obstructed Pulmonary Disease). Then she developed cancer of the liver. And finally – just a week or two before her daughter Elena, partner Lou and granddaughter Stella, were due to arrive from London – the dreaded cancer of the pancreas. She kept silent about her last diagnosis until they arrived.

She "passed away" in the presence of her daughter, Elena, just before midnight on the 27 August 2015. Elena and I had been spending alternate nights with Juliet in the Hospice. It was Elena's turn.

She is much lamented by family, friends, and colleagues around the world. Many of them have written and published touching tributes.

I miss her terribly.

Juliet in New York, aged 20

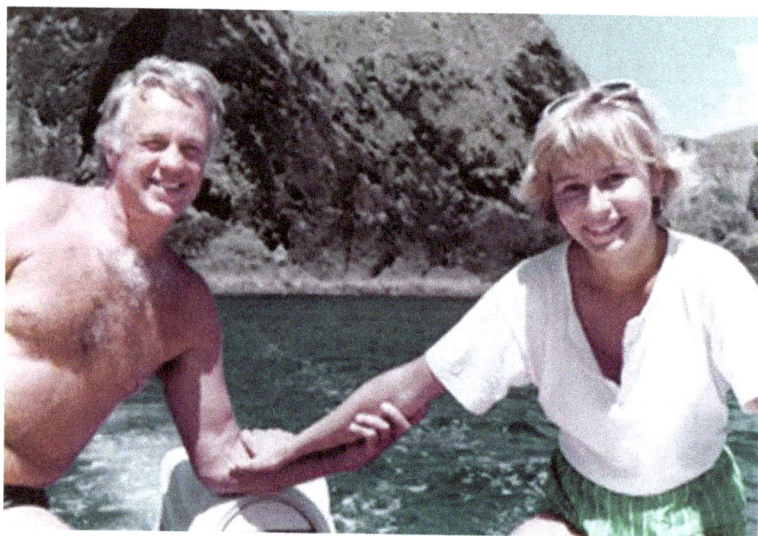

Above: Raymond and Ingrid, 1984

Below: Portrait of Ingrid, 1985

Juliet in 2001 on the day she and Ray were reunited

149

Juliet in the South of France

Above: Juliet on Whistler Mountain

Below: Juliet in Tanzania

Raymond and Juliet with his sons Gresham and Brett,
snowmobiling at Silver Star, BC

Raymond and Juliet, with sons Brett and Gresham, Gresham's partner Steve, and granddaughter Aleisha, Christmas Day, 2014